Berch
Obers

MW01480802

Hitler's Eagle's Nest

Written and researched by BRETT HARRIMAN

2014

©Map hand-drawn by Brett Harriman

map not to scale

Baltic Sea

North Sea

Kiel

Rostock

Hamburg

Berlin

Poland

Elbe R.

Neth.

Germany

Cologne

Dresden

Koblenz

Frankfurt

Czech Rep.

Prague

Trier

Mosel R.

Rhine R.

Rothenburg

Ceský Krumlov

Baden-Baden

Black Forest

Vienna

Freiburg

Munich

Chiemsee

Danube R.

France

Berchtesgaden

Füssen

Salzburg

Basel

Switz.

Innsbruck

Austria

Italy

Graz

Hungary

Slovenia

N

Harriman
TRAVEL BOOKS

Harriman Travel Books — travel publishing, February 2014.

ISBN: 978-0-6159772-6-3

Printed in the United States of America.

Hand-drawn maps created by © Brett Harriman.

Pictures used throughout the interior of this book were taken by © Brett Harriman, except for St. Bartholomew church on page 7 (courtesy of Bayerische Seenschifffahrt GmbH) and Brett sliding into the salt mines on page 5.

Cover created by © Brett Harriman.

Pictures on the front and back cover of this guide were taken by © Brett Harriman. *Selbstbedienung* on the front cover means "self service," i.e. simply pick out the pumpkin or flowers of your choice then drop the nominal cost into the coin slot directly above the "K" in *Kasse*.

Postmark stamp on front cover is dated (the European way) 06.06.2014, or June 6, 2014, the 70th anniversary of the Normandy ("D-Day") landings.

Although Harriman has exhaustively researched the latest information before press time, he accepts no responsibility for stolen street signs, schedule changes, union strikes, late trains, hangovers, overcooked schnitzel, traffic jams, lacking the use of common sense, bad weather, loss of property, inconvenience or injury sustained by any person using this guidebook. It is always prudent to be prepared and confirm all travel information before departure.

GPS data is provided for reference only. Harriman is not responsible for malfunctioning satellites or erroneous coordinates.

All comments, tips, suggestions, or whatever it is you want to get off your chest, please email to Europe@HarrimanTravelBooks.com

Berchtesgaden, Obersalzberg & Hitler's Eagle's Nest

Contents

This guidebook is updated every year. It is the very latest resource on Berchtesgaden, Obersalzberg, and the Eagle's Nest to hit the market. (In essence, there is no single regularly printed guidebook regarding these sites and attractions that is more current and comprehensive than this resource.) While many publishers of guidebooks update their material every so often, Harriman Travel Books is as consistent as the annual wildebeest migration in the Serengeti. Although some details will invariably change after the research has been logged, the vast majority of information is accurate and reliable. I personally visit the sites contained within this guidebook every autumn and therefore it is released with the utmost "freshness" for the coming year. Moreover, it is designed for you to travel like a local, to save time and money, to experience an enjoyable and authentic trip, while leading to new adventures and acquaintances along the way. Thank you for your support, and please tell others about "Harriman Travel Books" — Brett Harriman

Please note when using this guidebook, I've written all times using the 24-hour clock. Europeans exclusively use this system to keep time. Here are the conversions:

1:00 = 1 a.m.	13:00 = 1 p.m.
2:00 = 2 a.m.	14:00 = 2 p.m.
3:00 = 3 .a.m.	15:00 = 3 p.m.
4:00 = 4 a.m.	16:00 = 4 p.m.
5:00 = 5 a.m.	17:00 = 5 p.m.
6:00 = 6 a.m.	18:00 = 6 p.m.
7:00 = 7 a.m.	19:00 = 7 p.m.
8:00 = 8 a.m.	20:00 = 8 p.m.
9:00 = 9 a.m.	21:00 = 9 p.m.
10:00 = 10 a.m.	22:00 = 10 p.m.
11:00 = 11 a.m.	23:00 = 11 p.m.
12:00 = 12 p.m.	00:00 = midnight

©Brett Harriman

Berchtesgaden

"Wen Gott lieb hat, den lässt er fallen in dieses Land."
(Whom God loves, he places in this land.)

Population: 8,000. **Country-Area code:** +49-(0)8652.
Elevation: 530 m (1,740 ft). **License plate:** BGL (short for Berchtesgadener Land).

After the founding of Salzburg in 696 A.D. came the first mention of many settlements in the area, including the forest in front of the snow-peaked Watzmann (Germany's second-highest mountain at 2,712 m/8,900 ft).

In the 11th century, Lord Perther arrived and built a hunting cabin that became known as Perther's Gaden. From this moniker evolved the name Berchtesgaden.

In 1102, Augustinian monks settled here and began building a monastery with an adjoining church; look for the twin spires rising above town. The holy men were determined to achieve this symbolic feat as they had first proclaimed Perther's Gaden "…a terrifying forest constantly covered with ice and snow… a vast solitude inhabited by wild beasts and dragons," according to David Harper, co-founder of Eagle's Nest Historical Tours (see Tours below).

Frederick I (Barbarossa), Holy Roman Emperor and king of Germany from 1152-90, was delighted to hear of this fruitful monastery that neighbored the ever-annoying archbishops of Salzburg who boasted abundant deposits of salt. Barbarossa was quick to grant the monks extra rights to hunt, fish, forest, cultivate, and develop mines to excavate the "white gold" on their side of the border. Salt was the key resource in these parts that assured Berchtesgaden unusual power for such a small enclave, securing a political voice in the Reichstag (or parliament) and ultimately the right to become an independent principality ruled by prince-provosts. Even today salt remains king, accounting for a wealth of wellness centers and the official title of Kurgebiet, or health-resort region.

The following centuries brought social woes to the Catholic settlement: salt squab-

ORIENTATION

bles continued with Salzburg, the Thirty Years' War raged across Europe, and Protestant ways became covertly trendy.

In 1803, Napoleon dashed in with his battle-hardened *Grand Armée* and seized Berchtesgaden in one swoop. The monastery was consequently disbanded and church administration secularized. In the years to follow, Berchtesgaden was tossed around like a political football. First it was annexed to Salzburg under Habsburg rule before finally being restored to Bavaria in 1810. This attracted the Bavarian royal family who in 1818 refashioned the former monastery to a palace in which to relish the majesty of summer vacation in the lower Alps. (Perhaps Ludwig II garnered his fantastic inspirations in this idyllic corner of the kingdom while hiking alpine trails as a boy?)

The 20th century produced two world wars. The first was fought in the distant trenches of France and Belgium, but the second came knocking at Perther's front door. Adolf Hitler became chancellor of Germany in 1933 and decided to figuratively pitch his tent in the Gaden, calling it home. Hitler began the Second World War that Germany grossly lost. Thankfully, the Allied band of brothers safeguarded the hallowed Augustinian seat, securing its prosperity for centuries to come and *your* timely visit.

> 👍 **Don't miss it!:** I'd like you to experience as many of the attractions written in the Suggested Itinerary (below) as possible but if there is one sight you should not miss, it is the **Eagle's Nest** (page 35). With extra time set off on my self-guided **World War II bunker tour** (page 32). Last of all, there is one element you literally can't miss during your stay (unless bad weather prevails) and that is the **emerald-green** tinge accenting the local streams and rivers. This mesmerizing hue reflects the minerals (chiefly gypsum and limestone) washing in from the mountains.

Suggested Itinerary:

Sights: The big three blockbuster attractions in Berchtesgaden are the **salt mines** (page 5), **Eagle's Nest** at Obersalzberg (page 35), and **Königssee lake** in the national park (page 7). If you start first thing (9:00) in the morning (May-Oct), you can do all three in one day. If it's *sunny I'd begin with the Nest, then delve into the mines and conclude my day cruisin' Königssee. (Note that food is served at all three attractions, or simply roll out a picnic whenever, wherever.) *If it's overcast in the morning, do the mines first then the Nest (with the hope that the weather has cleared by the time you climb the mountain). If I had to pick only two of the three attractions to visit, I'd first choose the Eagle's Nest (at Obersalzberg because I'm a World War II buff) then Königssee (because there are other salt mines but there is only one lake in Central Europe most similar to a fjord).

In addition to the abovementioned attractions, consider a revitalizing visit to the **Watzmann Therme** for a vacation from your vacation (indulge in a swim, soak, Jacuzzi, full-body massage, page 10). With extra time, join the guided **mountain hiking** program offered *free* by the Nationalpark Berchtesgaden (see page 12, Nationalpark-Haus visitor's center) or on your own trek the untamed and unforgettable **Almbach Gorge** (page 13). Swing by the **Grassl Enzianbrennerei** for free samples of liqueur and schnapps (page 9). If you're visiting in winter and time it right, experience the **bobsled** thrill of a lifetime (page 8) or the forbidding custom that is **Krampus** (page 14).

Good Eats: Complement your Bavarian day with lunch or dinner at the **Goldener Bär** (daily 10:00-23:00, cash only) on the main pedestrian drag or for more money rocket up to the scenic outdoor **Panorama restaurant** on the rooftop of the newly built Hotel Edelweiss (page 16) in view of the Berchtesgadener Alps and Eagle's Nest. You could also try the traditional bill of fare and beer at Berchtesgaden's very own **Hofbräuhaus** (page 8) or with pleasant weather stop by the **restaurant Watzmann** (Franziskanerplatz 2, daily, last order 21:30, food specials posted out front, cash only) sit on the terrace and marvel majestic mountains with your meal. For Berchtesgaden's best Thai-Indian fusion jog over to **Kurz a Curry** at Schlossplatz 3 (Tue-Sat 17:00-00:00, June-Oct Monday also). For fast-food options, join on-the-go locals at the butcher (**Metzgerei Bösl**, Mon-Fri 7:30-18:00, Sat 7:30-12:30) next to the Goldener Bär. Order a meat plate (e.g. schnitzel, schweinebraten) or a grilled sausage on a bread roll, then mosey to the neighboring bakery (**Bäckerei Zechmeister**) and pick up something sweet to crown your picnic. **Drivers**, with nice weather (April-Oct) and a few hours to spare, turn to Ettenberg (page 15) in the Excursions section for a delicious culinary experience in the Alps.

☞ **Children:** Fun things kids enjoy to do, see and eat in Berchtesgaden are the **salt mines** (page 5); **Königssee lake** (page 7); **Watzmann Therme** (page 10); **Almbach Gorge** (page 13); sites at Obersalzberg: **zoo** (page 22), hike to **Mooslahnerkopf** (page 27), find the **Kampfhäusl** and **Theater** (page 29), explore a real WWII bunker (page 31), ride bus up to **Eagle's Nest** (page 35); lunch/dinner at **restaurant Watzmann** or **Metzgerei Bösl** and **Bäckerei Zechmeister** (see above).

Tourist Information, (www.berchtesgadener-land.info, Königsseer Strasse 2, tel. 08652/9670, June thru mid-Oct Mon-Fri 8:30-18:00, Sat 9:00-17:00, Sun 9:00-15:00—and mid-Oct thru May Mon-Fri 8:30-17:00, Sat 9:00-12:00). Berchtesgaden's main TI is located opposite the train station, on the other side of the traffic circle. Stop in for your free town map or to book a tour. Berchtesgaden's second TI (April-Sept Mon-Sat 9:00-18:00, Sun 10:00-13:00 & 14:00-18:00—and Oct-March Mon-Fri 9:00-18:00, Sat/Sun 10:00-13:00 & 14:00-18:00) is a small office situated inside the Kongresshaus, adjacent to the Franciscan church cemetery, opposite the main pedestrian zone in town.

   Tours: If you're interested in a personalized tour of the Eagle's Nest, Obersalzberg, World War II bunker system, or The Sound of Music sites, there's only one outfit to consider: **Eagle's Nest Historical Tours**, (www.eagles-nest-tours.com, tel. 08652/64971, CC: VC, MC, AE). The owners, David and Christine Harper, are a lovely husband-and-wife team who hail from the USA but who have called Berchtesgaden home since the '80s. Because I've known them since the '90s, I can personally say that the Harpers' booming success is attributed to their congenial personalities, in-depth tours, and wealth of local knowledge. (Pictured: Christine at the tour desk.) **Note:** Tours depart from the company tour desk located within Berchtesgaden's main tourist information office. Arrive at least 15 min before scheduled tour departure time. Due to the intense historical nature of the following Nest tour, bookings for children under the age of 6 are not accepted. The **Eagle's Nest Historical Tour** (mid-May thru Oct, daily 13:15, duration 4hr, max 30 persons, book ahead, adult 53€, student/senior 65+ or active-duty military 50€, youth 6-14yr 35€) includes all admission fees and a guided tour of the Eagle's Nest, Obersalzberg, and access to an underground bunker. The **Sound of Music tour** (Mon-Sat 8:30, duration 4hr, max 8 persons, book ahead, adult 40€, youth 6-11yr 30€, children under 6yr are free) revisits the sights in Salzburg made famous by this movie classic.

Emergency Tel. Numbers, valid free Germany-wide, dial **112** for general emergencies (like dialing 911 in the USA), or you can dial **110** for Police (Polizei).

Railers, Berchtesgaden is train-friendly but if you're coming from the north you'll have to transfer in Freilassing (German border town neighboring Salzburg). However, most of you wishing to visit Berchtesgaden will be coming from Salzburg, in which you have four options: train, bus, taxi, (pricey) tour. **By train:** If you're holding a Eurail consecutive-day or dated Flexi/Select pass, you ride free on the train: 85-min trip (hrly with one change). **By bus:** If you're not holding a discounted rail pass (and even if you are you may want to), forget the train and ride bus 840 from Salzburg to Berchtesgaden. It's quicker and cheaper, (see "Bus 840 to Berchtesgaden" page 41). **By taxi:** From Salzburg's main train station it will cost around 45€ to Berchtesgaden and 55€ to Obersalzberg. **Pricey tour:** If interested, tours are available to Berchtesgaden from Salzburg; ask TI or staff at your digs for the latest info.

Berchtesgaden's train station

(GPS: N47 37.562 - E12 59.949) was built in 1937 at a blinding pace in harmony with Third Reich improvements generated by a regime that had planned to dominate Europe. As the gateway to Hitler's neighborhood, Berchtesgaden received numerous foreign dignitaries and therefore the train station was designed to impress. After its completion, Berchtesgaden—an alpine community with just a few thousand residents—had a train station that was larger than the one in Athens, the capital of Greece. When Hitler would steam into town, on his train curiously called "Amerika," the mood bordered hysteria. Swastikas flapped from every window and flower-carrying children stood at the forefront of mesmerized crowds. Such was a typical scene in Nazi Germany when the Führer came to town. Today, things have quieted to a crawl; just 18 trains chug through the station daily and the only time local crowds get worked up is when Krampus (page 14) whips through the market square. **Note:** To store your things for a short period, **lockers** (1€-2€/24hr) at the train station are located on platform 1.

Outside the station, local buses head to all the sights and a queue of cabs wait patiently for business (**by taxi** it will cost about 12€ to Obersalzberg, 9€ to salt mines, 12€ to Königssee, 45€ to Salzburg, 250€ to Munich airport, .50¢ per luggage item, .50¢ to book a cab by phone: 08652/4041). Also outside the station's main entrance is an Apotheke, or **pharmacy** (Mon-Fri 8:00-19:00, Sat 8:00-14:00), and across the traffic circle is the **TI** (see previous page). Left of the station's front facade, 50 steps climb through an arched passage (marked **Zum Markt/Zentrum**) to a walkway leading over the tracks and into town.

Drivers/Parking: For street parking pay at nearby automat and leave ticket on dashboard of your car, .50¢/hr, max 2hr, applicable Mon-Fri 10:00-17:00, and Sat 10:00-13:00 with parking dial (page 42), free all other times. There are plenty of parking possibilities throughout Berchtesgaden. Free spaces can be had on the west side of town between the gas station and traffic circle at the former Berchtesgadener Hof site. **Note:** If you spend the night in Berchtesgaden you'll receive a Guest Card (Gästekarte), with which you're entitled to half-price parking around town, as well as at Obersalzberg (Eagle's Nest departure area) and Königssee, and in the neighboring community of Ramsau. For an über-scenic and **delicious culinary experience** (April-Oct) in the foothills of the Bavarian Alps, flip to Ettenberg (page 15) in the Excursions section.

Grocery Stores: Across the river from the main tourist information office you'll find two grocery stores (Mon-Sat 7:00-20:00), the more abundantly stocked **Rewe** and the discounted **Lidl**, where lovers of gummi bears will find Haribo cheaper. Note: At this location Rewe also has a Getränkemarkt, a separate building containing wholesale beverages (such as a wide assortment of wines and racks of beer).

Post Office: The post office (Mon-Tue and Thu-Fri 9:00-12:30 & 14:00-17:00, Wed 9:00-12:30, Sat 9:00-12:00) is located at Franziskanerplatz 2 in the center of town behind the restaurant Watzmann. **Note:** Pharmacy at train station sells postage stamps.

Coin Laundry: A coin laundry (Waschsalon, daily 8:00-19:00, May-Oct till 21:00, 3€/wash, 1€/dry 10 min, wash powder 1€ available from reception desk of next-door Hotel Wittelsbach) is located Maximilianstrasse 16, on the main road running through the center of town, a few doors up from the restaurant Watzmann.

SIGHTS

Note: Throughout this section and chapter I have listed the discount you will receive with the overnight Guest Card, page 16. (In short, if you stay the night in Berchtesgaden you'll be given a guest card, locally Gästekarte.)

Eagle's Nest, page 35.

Obersalzberg, Hitler's former neighborhood, page 20.

Salt Mines, locally Salzbergwerk, (daily May-Oct 9:00-16:50 last entry, Nov 2 thru April 11:00-14:50 last entry, except closed Nov 1, Dec 24-25 & 31, Jan 1, Good Friday and Whit Monday; adult 16€, student 18-25yr 14.50€, youth 4-16yr 9.50€ [under 4yr free], family 39€-44€, 3€ discount with valid Salzburg Card or .50¢ with overnight guest card, www.salzzeitreise.de, tel. 08652/60020). Since the year 1517, Berchtesgaden's alpine caverns have been a rich source of salt. Although the mines are still actively producing brine, another lucrative resource has since materialized: tourism. On average some 400,000 visitors descend upon the salt mines each year. Embarking on a subterranean adventure, tourists eagerly throw on the provided pair of reflective blue overalls (that appear more like a NASA space suit than duds worn by traditional miners)

Salzbergwerk Berchtesgaden 2001

and ride the narrow-gauge railway nearly half a mile (650m/2,132ft) deep into the mountain that keeps a constant temperature of 53F (12C), swoosh down slick slides (like yours truly pictured), navigate a salty lake, and some youngsters even go as far as to lick the sodium-rich tunnel walls that in many parts resemble taffy.

A tour of the mine takes about an hour, but that's once you get inside. Expect to wait anywhere from 15 minutes during low season and up to two hours in high season (July/Aug). **Suggestion:** You can minimize the wait time by purchasing your tickets online (go to www.salzreise.de, click for English, enter the number of persons in your group/family then click 'Continue,' select your arrival date, follow the prompts, enter your CC details then print the receipt to give to the cashier upon your arrival). If you're not able to book ahead and are faced with a long wait, you can kill time by moseying along the river and checking out the Watzmann Therme (page 10). Drivers can reduce the wait time by dropping someone off at the ticket cashier en route to parking the car. **Note:** The mines are not for claustrophobics; confined spaces abound! Climb above the glass-encased entrance to the new terrace for a terrific view. **To get there**—<u>GPS</u>: N47 38.248 E13 01.028 or Bergwerkstrasse 83—the salt mines are nestled along a pretty jade-green stream on Bergwerkstrasse, which runs off the main road connecting Berchtesgaden with Salzburg. **Railers, NOTE,** there are no taxis waiting at the salt mines, thus if you don't have one already pre-booked to pick you up (tel. 08652/4041), you need to march to the main highway and catch the hourly bus to Berchtesgaden's train station, where you then catch a bus onward to your next destination (e.g. Eagle's Nest or Königssee lake). **Railers, from** Berchtesgaden's train station, either walk 30 min to the mines or catch bus 840 or 848 (typically departing daily 9:15, 10:15, 12:15, 13:50, 15:15, also Mon-Fri 11:15, 13:20, 16:15) and tell driver to drop you off at "Salzbergwerk" (5-min ride, then short walk to mines, but first check bus return times to coordinate your pick-up); small groups consider a taxi (about 9€ one way, tel. 08652/4041, consider scheduling a pick-up time with the driver upon being dropped off or call 08652/4041 when ready to be picked up). **Railers, from** Salzburg's train station, catch bus 840 (page 41) and tell driver to drop you off at "Salzbergwerk" (then short walk to mines, but first check bus return times to coordinate your pick-up). **Drivers, if you're** coming from Salzburg, follow signs to Berchtesgaden. As you approach town follow Salzbergwerk signs (right) into the parking lot: about 3.50€ up to four hours, .60¢/hr thereafter. **Drivers, from** the center of Berchtesgaden, pass the pedestrian shopping zone and Hotel Edelweiss (left) and follow the road as it curves right. At the bottom of the hill turn left at the traffic light (direction Salzburg)—this is almost a U-turn. Now you're on Bergwerkstrasse. Pass the second set of lights and a short distance farther follow Salzbergwerk signs (left) into parking area: 3.50€ up to four hours, .60¢/hr thereafter. (If it's high season and you don't have a pre-reserved start time at the salt mines, turn right at the second set of lights and drop someone off to get in line for tickets while you park the car. After the drop-off, continue straight to the main road, turn left and follow Salzbergwerk signs right into the parking lot.)

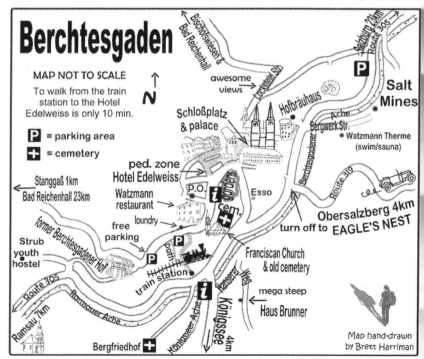

Königssee, (www.seenschifffahrt.de, tel. 08652/96360), boats run daily year round, mid-May thru Sept every 30 min 8:30-16:45 (July thru mid-Sept 8:00-17:15) and about every hour Oct thru April 9:30-15:45. Price (round trip to St. Bartholomew—35 min each way), adult 13.90€, youth 6-17yr 6.95€ (under 6yr free), family 34.80€, dog 3€; for more scenery and adventure, buy the ticket to Salet (summer only) at the far end of the lake.

Cool blue and magnificently photogenic, Königssee (meaning King's Lake) is one of Germany's cleanest lakes, secluded deep in the wilds of Berchtesgaden's 210 sq km (81 sq mi) national park treasured for its unspoiled beauty and nature trails. Königssee is the only lake in Central Europe most similar to a fjord, a long and narrow body of water flanked by vertical rock walls cut by an immense glacier during an ice age. What's more, Königssee is Bavaria's deepest lake at 192 m (630 ft); it is 8 km (5 mi) long; 1.25 km (.77 mi) at its widest point; and it is hemmed in on three sides by the Alps, including the snow-peaked Watzmann, which cast their dreamy reflection on the lake's resplendent surface. Königssee is so clear and clean that it boasts drinking-quality water, and the locals are intent on keeping it pure, thus swimming in the lake is atypical and the classic wooden boats that cruise across it are electrical. The 100-year-old Königsseer fleet of 17 boats quietly ship more than 700,000 people annually across the lake's emerald-green waters. (This intriguing color reflected by the sun is the result of minerals, primarily gypsum and limestone, washing into the lake from the mountains. Königssee feeds the streams and rivers in Berchtesgaden and therefore they, too, mirror this captivating color.) Most visitors disembark at St. Bartholomew to marvel its postcard-pretty church dating from medieval times. Midway into the cruise the captain stops the boat to blow his trumpet at the sheer cliffs prompting the "Königsseer echo." **Hikers** wander 90 min beyond St. Bartholomew to the Ice Chapel (page 13), and from the Königssee boat dock they trek to the dramatic vista at Painter's Corner (page 12). **Interestingly,** the lake rarely freezes over and therefore boats run daily year round. The last time the lake froze was during the winter of 2005-06. It was so cold, and the ice so thick, that people were allowed to walk and skate across the lake, but nobody reached St. Bartholomew quicker than the innkeeper who dared to drive his car there. Really!

Königssee is truly wunderbar; come experience it for yourself! That said, the clutter of kitschy souvenir shops and eateries, including a McDonald's, you have to pass to reach

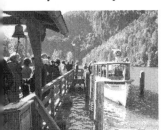

the lake and boat dock hardly complement the alpine setting. Oh, and the myriad ducks populating the shoreline would be very appreciative if you tossed a few bread crumbs their way. *Quack!* Romantics, seize the opportunity to row your partner around this stunningly beautiful setting (boat rental 2 pax 7€/hr, 4 pax 10€/hr, 40€/day, 50€ cash deposit, walk left of the Königssee dock to the wooden boat shed marked Ruderboote, mid-May thru beginning of October 11:00-17:00, otherwise closed). **Suggestion:** Plan your rendezvous with St. Bartholomew to coincide with an appetite for the freshly caught smoked trout (geraucht Forelle) served at the shoreline Fischerei (from 11:00, mid-April thru Oct). The owner, Thomas Amort, locally "der Fischermeister," upholds a family tradition of fishing on Königssee, a privilege granted exclusively to his ancestors centuries ago by

Berchtesgaden's prince-provosts. **SOM fans**, Königssee can be briefly seen during the aerial shots in the beginning of the film. **To get there**, <u>GPS</u>: N47 35.576 - E12 59.237, Königssee is located 5 km south of Berchtesgaden at the end of Königsseer Strasse, beginning opposite the train station. En route, your journey to the lake will be in view of the Eagle's Nest perched high above upon a pointy peak (to your left). **Drivers**, Königsseer Strasse ends at a pay parking lot, 4€ for day ticket (Tageskarte) or 2€ for holders of the overnight guest card (fees applicable daily 7:00-19:00). **Railers**, from Berchtesgaden's train station, bus 841 departs daily for Königssee (and the neighboring Jennerbahn) typically :15 min past every hour until late afternoon (10-min trip, upon arriving note pick-up times); small groups consider a taxi (about 12€ one way, tel. 08652/4041).

Bobsled & Luge, (www.weltcup-koenigssee.de). Right of the Königssee docks you'll see a track at the base of the forested mountainside, within a 10-min walk of the boat departure area. Beginning way up the mountain, this 1,300-meter-long (nearly 1 mile) ice canal was constructed in 1968 with the hopes of Berchtesgaden becoming an Olympic venue. At the time it was the first artificially frozen track in the world. Locally Kunsteisbahn, the Königssee ice canal combines the daring tempo of Formula 1 racing with the methodical proficiency of a championship round of golf at St Andrews. Its total obstacles include 16 curves and a drop of 10.35% with hair-raising track speeds reaching 130 kph, or 80 mph. Not surprisingly, the Kunsteisbahn today is the venue for international competitions as well as the training center for the German bobsled and luge teams. So if you ever see Germany win one of these icy events on TV, for example during the Winter Olympics, you now know where they train. In fact, Berchtesgaden is the national headquarters of the bobsled and luge (www.bsd-portal.de). More importantly, if you're visiting in winter (Nov thru mid-March) you can experience the same blinding rush, the **thrill of a lifetime**, riding in a 4-man Olympic bobsled here on the Königssee ice canal like all the other champions before you. Check with the TI in advance for the updated schedule or contact the organizer direct (tel. 08652/976-069, www.rennbob-taxi.de, 90€ per person and ride, 2€ discount with overnight guest card, 4-man bobsled is piloted by a professional and price includes a remembrance gift in addition to a certificate of achievement as bobsled co-pilot). You won't need to bring any special equipment other than a good pair of gloves and a large set of *cojones*! **Note:** Berchtesgaden isn't the only alpine venue to bob, Innsbruck also has an Olympic run you can challenge.

Hofbräuhaus, (daily 10:00-midnight, braeustueberl-berchtesgaden.de, 11€-15€ main dish, English menu available, CC: VC, MC, AE, tel. 08652/976-724). Established in 1645, this internationally recognized house of beer celebrates more than 365

years of brewing tradition in Berchtesgaden and is a delicious site to experience. Sit with locals in the house restaurant "Bräustüberl" or summer garden quaffing the golden nectar of Berchtesgaden (half liter 3.30€) and indulging in regional cuisine, like the Schweinshaxe. Consider the daily warm-cold buffet starting at 17:00 (pay for the dishes you choose). Also recommended is the Heimatabend (traditional Bavarian show, including whip cracking, dancing and spoon clanging) every *Friday at 20:00 end of May thru beginning of October, 5€/person (*check ahead as times may have changed). **To get there**, <u>GPS</u>: N47 38.060 E13 00.442, the HBH is situated at Bräuhausstrasse 13, just off the main road connecting Berchtesgaden with Salzburg, within a 10-min walk of the town center, or two stops on either bus [1]837, [2]840, or [2]848 from the train station (tell driver to drop you off at [1]"Hofbräuhaus" or [2]"Watzmann Therme," then short walk). Drivers, park in their lot.

Grassl Enzianbrennerei, distillery, (Mon-Fri 9:00-17:00, Sat 9:00-12:00 but May-Oct Mon-Fri 9:00-18:00 and Sat 9:00-16:00, allow 20-45 min for a visit, www.grassl.com, tel. 08652/95360, CC: VC, MC). Over 180,000 visitors per year stop by this quintessentially Bavarian attraction for a free look into Germany's oldest En-

zian distillery, established in 1602. The distillers at Grassl use the root of the Enzian mountain flower as the essential ingredient to produce their signature liqueur and schnapps. And—get this (providing you're not the driver)—you can sample up to 30 Grassl blends for *free!* No doubt you'll appreciate at least one from the bunch, which can be purchased by the bottle, and many can even be bought in mini shot bottles (1€ each but get one free with over-night guest card) that make *excellent* souvenir-gifts for friends back home. One of Grassl's more potent yet popular blends is the herbal liqueur Bergfeuer, or "mountain fire," containing 57% alcohol by volume; perhaps explaining why most everyone in town is seemingly in a good mood. Or maybe it's the potato schnapps (referred to as Bavarian vodka 38% abv), or the cherry liqueur (Kirschlikör 25%

abv), or the unique tasting chocolate-chili liqueur (17% abv). **Suggestion:** Upon your arrival look for the pictured manager Karsten Brust (who speaks good English) and ask him if it's possible to view the 10-min orientation film in English. (The scenery in this film is breathtaking.) If you're a large family or a group of folks, call Karsten in advance (tel. 08652/953-629) to schedule a viewing time and to ask if he has an opening for a brief tour of the distillery. Meanwhile, have fun sampling, shopping, and strolling through the traditional alpine cabin. **To get there,** <u>GPS</u>: N47 39.382 E13 02.486, Grassl is located at Salzburgstrasse 105, 4 km from Berchtesgaden and 18 km from Salzburg on route 305 running between the two communities. **Drivers,** free parking out front. **Railers,** catch the hourly bus 840 from either Berchtesgaden or Salzburg's train station and tell driver to drop you off at "Enzianbrennerei." **Note:** Time-crunched travelers can experience the same Enzian effect from Grassl's store on Schloßplatz in the center of town, Mon-Fri 9:00-18:00, Sat 9:00-16:00.

Schloßplatz, <u>GPS</u>: N47 38.026 E13 00.178. Spread beneath the twin spires rising above town is Schloßplatz, or Palace Square, a spacious pedestrian plaza home to the blessed Stiftskirche, or **Collegiate Church**, where the Augustinian monks established Berchtesgaden more than 900 years ago. Adjoining the church is the former Augustinian

monastery, dating from 1122. This significant salmon-shaded structure was later converted to the seat of Berchtesgaden's prince-provosts and from 1818-1918 it was used as a summer residence by the Bavarian royal family, Wittelsbach. Thus, the fairy-tale king, Ludwig II, spent many a summer day here in his youth. Penciled on one of the palace doorframes, for example, a line measures the future king's height at the age of six. Today, these palatial digs, locally Königliches Schloss, or **Royal Palace**, are still used by members of the Wittelsbach clan when in town (generally for two weeks mid-August at which time the palace will be closed to visitors). The Königliches Schloss makes for a splendid rainy day attraction but because the palace is privately owned and occasionally occupied, visitors must join the 50-min guided tour (in German but free translation sheet available, mid-May thru mid-Oct, Sun thru Fri 10:00-12:00 & 14:00-16:00, rest of year Mon-Fri 11:00 & 14:00, adult 9.50€, student [12-25yr] 4€, family 19€, 1€ discount with overnight guest card, www.haus-bayern.com, tel. 08652/947-980). Within the arched colonnade on Schloßplatz is a **memorial** to Berchtesgaden's war dead, their names, chiseled into rose-marble tablets, span two world wars. Painted on the above facade are 15 figures, three of these are Wehrmacht soldiers, one lay mortally wounded while a woman grieves over his body. Gothic typeface reads (left) "The fallen sons of Berchtesgaden"; (right) "They gave their lives; their sacrifice will always be remembered." On a more festive note, return here in December when the snow-white square is ornamented with the gingerbread-scented Christmas market. Mmm.

Watzmann Therme, (www.watzmann-therme.de, daily 10:00-22:00, Fri-Sat till midnight, adult 10.50€/2hr, stay longer and pay 1.50€/30 min or better 14€/4hr, 15.50€/day pass, youth 6-15yr 6€/2hr or 11€/day pass, child 2-5yr 2.50€/2hr or 4.50€/day pass (under 2yr free), family 35€/4hr, sauna 5€ extra, discount available with valid Bayern-Ticket and overnight guest card, towel hire 2.50€ and 15€ deposit; **back massage** 23€/20 min, **full-body massage** 40€/40 min, other options available, best to book by phone at least 48hr in advance: tel. 08652/946-450). It's easy: just show up, pay admission, get rejuvenated! Similar to the Caracalla spa in Baden-Baden, the Watzmann Therme spoils its clientele with a plethora of waterworks and remedial stations, such as massaging waterfalls and salt inhalation rooms, Finnish and herbal saunas, whirlpools and solariums, a surge channel and half-sized Olympic pool, therapeutic sodium bath and nutritious poolside restaurant, and an 80-meter-long (262 ft) waterslide called the Black Hole. Yikes! Outside, patrons relax on lounge chairs and soak up the sunshine with Alpine views while sauna-goers parade between cabins in their birthday suits. **Note:** All saunas, per usual in Germany, are totally nude. Mondays, all day, are reserved for women-only in the saunas, unless it's a holiday. **To get there**, the Watzmann Therme is located at Bergwerkstrasse 54, near the salt mines. **Drivers**, use the same directions to the salt mines but instead (if you're coming from the center of Berchtesgaden turn right at the second set of traffic lights and) park out front of the Watzmann Therme. **Railers**, use the same directions to the salt mines but instead it's a 25-min walk from the train station or by bus (no matter from Berchtesgaden or Salzburg) tell the driver to drop you off at "Watzmann Therme," then short walk.

Berchtesgadener Hof: (This site no longer exists; it has been razed.) Most World War II buffs are familiar with the Berchtesgadener Hof from its portrayal in the television miniseries "Band of Brothers," episode 10, "Points," when the boys of Easy Company entered the hotel and began lifting Hitler souvenirs.

Originally called the Grand Hotel from its inauguration in 1898, these digs once pampered European nobility. When the Nazis acquired the hotel in the 1930s, they renovated it and changed the name to Berchtesgadener Hof. The property fast became the preferred digs of Hitler's guests, including

General Irwin Rommel ("Desert Fox"), British Prime Minister Neville Chamberlain, Heinrich Himmler, Josef Goebbels, and Eva Braun before she moved in to the Berghof with Hitler on Obersalzberg.

Following World War II, the hotel was acquisitioned by U.S. forces and used as an R&R (AFRC) resort until 1995, when it was returned to the German authorities. After a decade of neglect, the building was razed (Nov 2006) to make way for the **Haus der Berge** (see Hiking on next page), the new 19€ million national park visitor's center. **Note:** The two pictures show the Berchtesgadener Hof in its derelict state in

2001 and again in 2007 after its removal (only back wall remaining). I snapped the latter picture from where the front entrance used to be, i.e. to bicyclist's left across road.

SIGHTS

Paula Hitler is unofficially buried in Berchtesgaden. If interested, turn to page 41.

Berchtesgaden's oldest cemetery, locally Alter Friedhof, situated at

the Franciscan church across from the restaurant Watzmann in the center of town, dates from the 17th century and accommodates a breadth of memorial markers, well-tended plots and tall, dignified tombstones maintained by relatives of the deceased. After Mass, look for family gatherings around plots to honor loved ones. Just inside the gate (closest to church), the first grave on the right is that of **Anton Adner** (pictured), b. 1705, d. 1822. At 117 years, Adner is recognized as Bavaria's oldest man. They say Adner's secret was walking, and his hobby was to knit warm garments and craft wooden toys for kids. You see, in those days, goods were taxed when crossing borders, unless they could be transported on your person. Thus Adner strapped a specially made wooden box to his back to carry his handiwork to distant markets to sell. During these journeys, Adner would knit socks and carve figurines as he went. Not surprisingly, the Bavarian king heard of Adner's remarkable story and at the mature age of 113 he was honored as one of the 12 worthiest men in the kingdom. According to tradition, this warranted a trip to the palace in Munich for the annual "washing of the feet" by the king on Maundy Thursday, the Thursday before Easter, which is symbolic of Jesus washing the feet of his disciples. For the next four years, Adner was invited to Munich for a royal scrub until his death in 1822. Opposite Adner's grave, **memorial markers** embedded in the wall remember Berchtesgaden's heroic sons. Their names and living dates span two world wars, inscribed for all to see: where they fell in combat, what year, their age. Some have a poem; most feature a black-and-white photo of a proud soldier in uniform. Many families lost two young men, some lost three (pictured, Lochner boys). One marker memorializes a father and his son, Josef Ponn senior and junior. Near the far end of the wall stands a large, featureless tombstone with the lone inscription:

Dietrich Eckart. This was Hitler's mentor—you can blame this guy for bringing the aspiring dictator to Berchtesgaden and, consequently, its dark Nazi legacy at Obersalzberg.

HIKING

Locals tell me, Berchtesgaden and its national park is one of God's greatest creations. Unsurprisingly, this place of natural wonder embraces a marveling multitude of hiking trails waiting for you to discover. Below I've researched a short list of scenic hikes for you to mull, from easy to adventurous. But the best way to get a grip on the magnitude of possibilities, as well as gaining a better understanding of the region and its geology, is to stop by the **national park visitor's center Haus der Berge** (former site of the Berchtesgadener Hof page 10, daily 9:00-17:00, tel. 08652/979-0600, www.nationalpark-berchtesgaden.de, located at Hanielstrasse 7, on the road running west from the center of town, within a 15-min trek from the train station. Note: The visitor's center and national park are free to enter). Come to this modern and revealing facility to learn about the Berchtesgaden National Park, from enchanting hikes to mountain huts and from environmental research to mapping geologic time. Germany's only national park in the Alps was established in 1978 and covers 210 sq km (81 sq mi), basically everything south of Berchtesgaden to the Austrian border, including the lakes Königssee and Hintersee. To get a better idea of the park's location would be to imagine the lower right corner of Germany on a map: The entire bottom half of the fist punching into Austria is the park. **Note:** Also in the Haus der Berge you'll find **free toilets**, a resplendent selection of English-language pamphlets, and the 'alpine kitchen' restaurant (Alpenküche, daily 9:00-18:00) with scenic terrace in view of the Berchtesgadener Alps. Novice hikers, get the updated schedule on the **free "wander program"** (led by a park ranger, summer and winter, no reservation necessary), and experienced hikers should pick up the brochure listing the Berghütten (mountain huts) that populate the higher elevations.

Berchtesgaden to Königssee: This walk is **easy and flat**, taking 90 min. Start on the (asphalt) path beginning across the river from Berchtesgaden's TI; (look to brown wooden sign pointing Königssee 5km; the second sign reads: Fußweg zum Königssee). The footpath mostly parallels the Königsseer Ache (stream) to Königssee lake (page 7). There are a number of food options at the lake but few en route to it. Consider riding the bus back to Berchtesgaden (check pick-up times upon arriving).

Königssee/Painter's Corner & Waterfall:
(For info on Königssee flip to page 7). This hike ranks **easy to adventurous**, requiring some 15 min to reach the **must-see** Painter's Corner, locally Malerwinkel (pictured), and about another 20 min to the waterfall. From the Königssee boat dock, mosey left; the road will turn to a trail climbing into the mixed alpine forest. Continue past Café Malerwinkel and the trail will soon drop into Painter's Corner, where you'll be rewarded with a glori-
ous view to St. Bartholomew and the far end of shimmering Königssee. (There are a few benches here to plop down on and relish your picnic.) Note: The next section to the waterfall can be *treacherous*, thus it is only suggested for sure-footed, experienced hikers who choose to proceed at their *own* risk. From Painter's Corner follow the path as it narrows down to the lake. Wander along the shoreline, sometimes while balancing on rocks and logs, and up to the cascading waterfall (Wasserfall, say Vasser-fall). The route is not signposted, thus you may have to ask a fellow hiker en route. Beware of the steep climb up to the main pool. The views will astound you, even outshining Painter's Corner. Funny story: When I was there a handful of German twenty-somethings arrived, stripped to their birthday suits, and soaked in the pool. Now that's genuine nature.

Königssee/Ice Chapel (Eiskapelle; for info on Königssee flip to page 7). The so-called Ice Chapel is an intriguing yet tough to find, freezing-cold and hazardous cave that develops a dome of ice during winter then dramatically melts by late summer. Although the 90-min trek leading to it is **scenic and rather unproblematic**, the Ice Chapel itself can be dangerous to explore on account of warm-weather conditions altering its size and shape (season to season) causing the ground to be unstable. Thus the authorities recommend that it *not* be entered. The trail begins at St. Bartholomew by the National Park info point. From here, the path leads to the Chapel of St. Johann and Paul at the footbridge before climbing through the forest to a large avalanche snow field at the foot of the Watzmann's east wall. When you're done, hop back on the boat to Salet (summer only) and immerse yourself in the majesty of Obersee and its delicious and dramatic scenery.

Almbach Gorge, locally Almbachklamm, (May-Oct daily 8:00-19:00, otherwise closed, adult 3€, youth 6-16yr 1.50€, .50¢ discount with overnight guest card, www.marktschellenberg.de). This marvelous trek is **easy to intermediate**, 90 min to 3 hours, depending on the route you choose. Located some 5 km from Berchtesgaden, the picturesque Almbach Gorge (Almbachklamm) is home to Bavaria's oldest marble mill (Kugelmühle, dating from 1683), the starting point of the hike. At length the path is about 3 km (2 mi), has 29 footbridges, and more than 300 steps with an elevation differential of about 200 m (650 ft). Wander past roaring waterfalls and pristine pools, through rock tunnels, along a gaping gorge swimming with Bachforelle (brook trout). **Suggestion:** At footbridge 17 (yes, the bridges are numbered) go right and follow the sign to Wallfahrtskirche Ettenberg; the incline steeply leads to the hamlet of (www.)Ettenberg(.de) and its quaint Baroque church (dating from 1725) parked on an idyllic plateau boasting postcard-pretty views of the valley and Alps (taking roughly 3 hours round trip from the marble mill). Plan your hike to go with a picnic or better yet (neighboring the Ettenberg church) try the traditional Gasthaus Mesnerwirt run by the Weinmann family for some 30 years (closed Monday). With extra time (1-2 hours), you have a couple of wonderful hiking opportunities to extend your journey from Ettenberg (ask a local to point the way). **To get there**, the Almbach Gorge is located 5 km from Berchtesgaden (left side of road) and 17 km from Salzburg on route 305 running between the two communities. **Railers**, catch the hourly bus 840 from either Berchtesgaden or Salzburg's train station and tell the driver to drop you off at "Almbachklamm," then 5-min walk (cross bridge and turn left—at the end of this narrow two-way road is the Almbach). **Drivers**, from Berchtesgaden, take the main road (route 305) direction Salzburg and after a handful of km follow the Almbachklamm sign pointing left (cross bridge and turn left—at the end of this narrow two-way road is the Almbach). If you're coming from Salzburg, it's just past Marktschellenberg on the right (then follow aforesaid directions over bridge).

Ice Cave, locally Eishöhle, (www.eishoehle.net, mid-May thru Sept daily 10:00-16:00 & Oct 10:00-15:00, otherwise closed, adult 7€, youth 6-16yr 4€, family 16€, .50¢ discount with overnight guest card, price includes 45-min guided tour, typically in German, departing at the top of every hour; allow at least 7 hours for a visit to/fro ice cave). This is a **steep hike**, an all-day adventure, requiring 3 hours to reach Germany's largest ice cave, located at an elevation of 1,570 m (5,150 ft) two-thirds up Untersberg mountain. Dress warm (meaning keep an extra sweater in your backpack), the cave is literally freezing and the walls are made of solid ice several meters thick. *Burrr.* At the start of the hike you'll ramble past a piece of medieval history, the Wehrturm (visible from the road). Dating from 1252, this former border tower (pictured)

HIKING

housed guards responsible for checking the IDs of people traffic as well as levying taxes on the passage of goods. From this point on your job is to move your buttocks in an upwardly direction. Above the tree level you'll reach the full-service mountain hut (Toni-Lenz-Hütte, open daily), affording food and drink and accommodations (12 beds, reservation required if you wish to stay the night, Austria tel. +43-[0]681/1027-0291). From the hut, the ice cave is roughly 20 min farther. Plan your hike to go with a picnic or sample the goodies at the hut, or do both. **To get there**, the starting point begins at the 13th-century customs tower, 1 km inside the Bavarian border with Austria. **Railers**, catch the hourly bus 840 from either Berchtesgaden or Salzburg's train station and tell the driver to drop you off at "Eishöhle." **Drivers**, from Berchtesgaden, take the main road (route 305) direction Salzburg. A short distance beyond the village of Marktschellenberg park in the dirt lot on the right (cross road and climb path to tower and beyond). If you're coming from Salzburg, park in the dirt lot on the left some 800 meters after crossing the Bavarian border (cross road and climb path to tower and beyond).

EVENTS & FESTIVALS 2014

May Day, May 1 (Thursday). This day is special throughout Bavaria because numerous communities (visit TI to find out which ones) will be raising their time-honored Maypole. May Day festivities include folk dancing, pole-climbing events, traditional costume, and customary beer drinking. Amen! Note that some communities postpone festivities a week or two. Thus, if you plan it right, you can follow the celebrations all month.

Pentecost (Whit) Monday, June 9. In Berchtesgaden, the salt miners have adopted this holiday as their own. (Consequently, the salt mines will be closed.) Led by members of the Collegiate Church, the salt miners wear traditional costume and parade through the decorated streets of town to Schloßplatz where a service will be held. Afterward, the procession continues.

Almabtrieb—(typically end of Sept, beginning of Oct)—is the Bavarian term for when the cows are led from their summer pastures to their winter stalls, which predictably transpires in the latter half of September. Milkmaids and cow herders adorn their livelihood with flamboyant headdresses and parade them along village streets to their homes. During this procession the milkmaids call out: "In God's name move on, my cow, in health and joy—St. Anthony will herd you." Truly a memorable spectacle to witness. It's especially interesting to see the resplendent cows being offloaded from specially made boats at Königssee and marched home past a throng of captivated crowds. Don't forget your camera. Inquire at the TI for exact locations and dates, which vary depending on weather.

Christmas Market, traditionally held on the market square during Advent weekends (13:00-19:00), including Friday, and all the weekdays leading up to Dec 24.

Krampus, (typically 5th & 6th of December, early evening). Exclusive to the alpine region is Krampus, a tradition dating from medieval times that kick-starts the Christmas season. The Krampus are essentially Santa's evil servants; more precisely a group of wicked-looking creatures (Kramperl, Buttnmandl and Gangerl) who accompany St. Nicholas through town before Christmas to frighten misbehaved children into being good. But, today, what really happens is the creatures run wild through Berchtesgaden's pedestrian zone whipping and terrorizing the populace at large. Although, legend does maintain that a generous whipping ensures good health and prosperity for the coming year, in addition to expelling all possible demons from your soul. Yikes! (To read how

German children in the remainder of the country observe St. Nicholas' feast day, see my Frankfurt guide.)

The whips (or switches) the Krampus carry are nothing to laugh at; each is handmade from a bundle of long and firmly woven plant stems, tied and taped together for maximum effect. Ouch! Each creature will arm itself with three to four switches in case one comes apart (i.e. unravels), or even more troubling, one gets snatched by a daring member of the public. The Krampus creatures are: **Kramperl**; boys wearing self-made fur costumes with handcrafted masks and modest bells attached to their belts. **Buttnmandl**; men wearing hand-carved masks, 3-6 large cowbells tied to their backs, and straw outfits that take an hour to don. **Gangerl** (pictured); this is the devil and the leader of the pack. He wears horns, a fur jacket, and a terrifying mask. Be afraid boys and girls. Be *very* afraid! (This alarming creature is perhaps why crime is so low in these parts.) Suggestion: Because the Krampus creatures tend to administer a painful whipping, wear ski pants (if you have 'em) or two pairs of jeans to help absorb the sting (in case you were to get stung). For a memorable experience, and a great souvenir, snatch one of the creatures' handmade switches. Only kidding.

EXCURSIONS

Besides hiking (page 12) and Obersalzberg (page 20), there are two other worthwhile jaunts I'd like to tell you about. The first concerns delicious scenery in the foothills of the Bavarian Alps and the second points to, arguably, Germany's most picturesque church.

Ettenberg: (This excursion is easiest for Drivers and doubles as a dreamy lunch idea, April-Oct, taking as little as 45 minutes round trip by road or several hours with lunch and hiking.) For a memorable and über-scenic culinary experience in the foothills

running up to Untersberg mountain, **Drivers** turn into the town of Marktschellenberg (by Austrian border) and climb the road to Ettenberg (5km). The road is narrow and full of curves, wending through velvety alpine pastures and evergreen forests to the quaint Baroque church at Ettenberg (pictured), nestling on an idyllic plateau next to the traditional *Gasthaus **Mesnerwirt** (closed Monday, tel. 08650/245, www.ettenberg.de), boasting panoramic views of the valley and mountains. (*After driving some 5km you'll reach a significant parking area flanked by woods; from here, the church and gasthaus are only one kilometer farther up the road. If the small graveled parking area opposite the Mesnerwirt is full, either wait for a space or return to the lot in the woods and hike back.) **Hikers**, you can reach Ettenberg and its scenic splendor by way of the Almbach Gorge (page 13).

Ramsau: (This excursion is easy for both Drivers and Railers, taking as little as 45 minutes round trip by car and one hour by bus.) Some 10km from Berchtesgaden is the town of Ramsau and its postcard-pretty Baroque church St. Sebastian (pictured below), dating from 1512, the focus of artists, professional photographers and shutterbugs alike. Right of the gate leading into the church cemetery is a fountain running beneath an antlered deer accenting a memorial listing the names of Ramsauer sons who fell during the two world wars. **Drivers**, from in front of the Berchtesgaden train station, head west on

route 305 to Ramsau. Continue into town; the church is straight ahead (right side) with
the stream and few parking spaces on the left.
Railers, from Berchtesgaden's train station, ride
bus 846 (typically departing :15 past the hour until
18:15) direction Hintersee and get off at Ramsau
Kirche (15-min trip). From here, skip across the
road and check return times. If all you want to do
is take a few quick pictures of the church, ride the
next bus back to Berchtesgaden typically departing :55 past the hour, giving you 25 minutes for a
visit (thus your whole trip will take about an hour).

GOOD SLEEPS

In Berchtesgadener Land, hoteliers must assess a nominal **bed tax** (2.10€ per adult per
night, 1.10€ 6-16yr) to its room rates. Although this sounds negative to your budget, it
could easily add up to a positive. That's because each overnight guest (from 6 years old)
will receive a **Guest Card** (Gästekarte) upon check-in. You see, the guest card entitles
the holder to select discounts around town and the region, including free use of the public bus system (RVO, plus reduced fare to Salzburg 4€ rt adult); 1.50€ off admission to
Eagle's Nest (page 35); .50¢ off Documentation Center (page 21); .50¢ off salt mines
(page 5); 10% off Watzmann Therme (page 10); 50% off parking at Königssee (page 7)
and Eagle's Nest departure area (page 37); .50¢ off both Almbach Gorge and Ice Cave
(page 13); free 20 ml shot bottle at Grassl Enzianbrennerei (page 9); 1€ off Royal Palace
(see Schloßplatz page 9); 1.10€ off Dürrnberg luge (see my Salzburg guide); around 15%
off Burg Hohenwerfen (see my Salzburg guide); and 1.50€ off Deutsches Museum (as
well as its two partner museums) in Munich (see my Munich guide).

    Note: Because Berchtesgaden is small-town Bavaria, many shops and eateries only
accept cash—no credit cards—thus at a money machine be sure to withdraw enough
funds to cover the essentials and more during your bucolic stay.

Note that my rudimentary rating system is based on the price of double occupancy.
    $ — pocket-friendly, 60€ or less.
    $$ — moderately priced, generally between 60€ and 100€.
    $$$ — upper end, generally between 100€ and 170€.
$$$$ — superior, from 180€.

$$$$ **Hotel Edelweiss,** (Maximilianstrasse 2, www.edelweiss-berchtesgaden.
com, tel. 08652/97990, **free Wi-Fi** in lobby, free high-speed Internet in room—get con-
nection cable from reception). Sprawling along the main pedestrian drag in the center of
town, this 4-star non-smoking spa hotel has been the
talk of Berchtesgaden since it's opening May 2010. If
you're not on a budget, stay here! The massive 38-mil-
lion-euro Hotel Edelweiss took 14 months to construct,
featuring 126 contemporary rooms (11 suites, 115 double rooms in six categories); a pair of restaurants
(ground floor café-eatery with pizzeria daily 11:00-mid-
night, and the rooftop Panorama restaurant with breathtaking 360-degree views daily 11:00-22:00); and in the
basement you'll discover the romantic alpine-themed

wine bar Weinstüberl (Fri-Sat 20:00-02:00). In addition to the regional cuisine and culture, you can jump up to the rooftop terrace for a swim in the glass-encased pool or soak in the outdoor Jacuzzi virtually within arm's reach of Berchtesgaden's spectacular snow-peaked Alps. On a clear day, the vista and mood from the terrace is nothing short of magnificent. If you desire more, get rejuvenated at the in-house spa affording a multitude of wellness facilities (e.g. for massages, mud baths, manicures, pedicures, facial treatments) and five sauna-steam baths (which 4 of 5 are nude). And hotel management have not neglected the concerns of parents, who can indulge in stress-free sightseeing while their children participate in a safe and coordinated program of daily adventure, arts and crafts and playtime under the watchful eyes of a staff member (free for children ages 3 and up; children under the age of 3 a baby-sitting service is provided for 10€/hr). Check the hotel website for family packages or last-minute deals. Do yourself a favor: for a handful more euros reserve a type "D" room in view of the Eagle's Nest. (Pass on the smaller room types A & B; types C & F are fine but may not be in view of the Eagle's Nest and type E is a suite.) **PRICE** (includes hearty buffet breakfast; all room types are quoted for double occupancy—query reception for rate of third/fourth person as well as for single use): room **type "A"** (25 sq m) 188-198€; room **type "B"** (30 sq m) 200-212€; room **type "C"** (35 sq m) 212-224€ (type C has the option of bathtub or shower and many of this room type face the Eagle's Nest but not all, thus you must request it upon booking); room **type "D"** (40 sq m) 224-236€ (all D rooms typically have both a bathtub and shower and face the Eagle's Nest); room **type "E"** (50-60 sq m) suite 256-268€; room **type "F"** (40 sq m, 224-236€) is a comforting choice based on the ancient Chinese Feng Shui style. All major CCs accepted. **Note:** Check-in from 15:00; check-out by 11:00. The higher room rate is roughly mid-May thru mid-Oct and New Year's. Children ages 0-6 stay free (except 80% discount in a suite), 7-11yr receive roughly 65% off, 12-16yr 45%. All beds here are twins set together to form a double. If it is a twin you're after, request when booking that the beds be separated. Consider the hotel's substantial **5-course dinner** with themed buffets, fresh salad bar, and all-you-can-eat ice cream (18:30-21:00, adult 25€, 12-16yr 12€, 7-11yr 7€, 0-6yr free, vegetarian, gluten-/lactose-free options available). **Drivers**, parking 4€/24hr; unload out front or below in the garage (then ride elevator to lobby). **Railers**, from the train station, the hotel is a 10-min trek but with weighty luggage spring for a cab (about 6€ plus .50¢/bag). By foot: exit station, go right toward corner then right through arched passage (marked Zum Markt/Zentrum), climb steps, cross walkway leading over tracks, hike path up, ahead go right at fork to street, then go right down to the pedestrian zone and your digs on the left.

$ **Haus Brunner,** (Hansererweg 16, tel. 08652/61886, little English spoken, **no In-**

ternet access). Figuratively a world away from the 4-star facilities and room rates mentioned above at Hotel Edelweiss, bed-and-breakfast Haus Brunner is amiably run by Herr and Frau Lösel who offer clean homely rooms with a balcony and stupendous views from its perch high above Berchtesgaden. Even from the breakfast table the alpine vistas are, literally, jaw-dropping! Don't let it discourage you that the shower and toilet facilities are positioned in the hallway; Haus Brunner is nonetheless a terrific, pocket-friendly choice in the home of locals. **PRICE**, Sgl 20€, Dbl 40€. GPS: N47 37.570 E13 00.157. **To get there**; across from the TI is Hansererweg; follow this road *up* to No. 16. Initially the road is flat, then it curves to the right and climbs at a grueling 24% grade! Jeepers; Hansererweg has got to be Germany's steepest neighborhood street. (My little

Smart rental car pictured in the driveway barely made it up the hill in 1st gear.) **Drivers**, beware—Hansererweg is two-way! **Railers**, call ahead and they may pick you up from the station. That said, to walk up the hill every time you return to your room may *not* be worth it.

$ **Hostel Strub,** [HI] (Struberberg 6, www.berchtesgaden.jugendherberge.de, **free Wi-Fi**, tel. 08652/94370, reception attended Mon-Fri 7:00-12:00 & 15:00-22:00, Sat/Sun 7:00-10:30 & 15:00-22:00). Dating from the late 1930s and containing 265 beds in two buildings, this extensive newly renovated hostel popular with school groups is found nestling in a small park reserve on the edge of town, 2 km from the train station. From the hostel's front door is a sharp view of the Eagle's Nest; a great angle to justify why British bombers missed their target on April 25, 1945. A mere javelin throw from the hostel is Strub Kasern, home base of the illustrious Gebirgsjäger, or elite "Edelweiss" mountain troops. **PRICE** (includes sheets and breakfast but add an extra 2.10€ per person per night for bed tax), dorm bed 25.40€, Sgl/Dbl available, family discount available. CC: VC, MC. **Note:** Non HI members add 3.10€ extra per night to the listed prices; guests 27 years of age or older add 4€ extra per night. If you're only staying one night, an extra 2€ will be assessed to the rate. Dorm rooms are separated by gender. Check-in 15:00-22:00 (but if you arrive earlier there's usually a staff member around). Hearty all-you-can-eat dinner specials 17:30-19:00. GPS: N47 37.449 E12 58.774. **Drivers**, from the train station, follow "by foot" directions below. **Railers**, from Berchtesgaden's train station, ride bus 839 to Jugendherberge (buses departing Mon-Fri 10:15 and 14:15, Sat/Sun 10:15 take 8 min, all other departures take around 25 min) or walk 30 min. **By foot:** Exit station right and walk the main road (Ramsauerstrasse) roughly 1 km and make the first right, direction Strub. Follow the Jugendherberge sign left up the hill. After a (600-meter) hike that will either make you feel twice your age or fit as a Gebirgsjäger, you'll see the hostel on the left.

$ **Leyererhof,** (Alpenstrasse 114, www.leyererhof.de, tel. 08657/371). Located 10 km from Berchtesgaden in the lush meadows running up to the toes of the Alps, these dreamy farmhouse-style digs are recommended for Drivers. If you're lucky enough to secure a vacancy, stay at least two nights. This Alpine neighborhood features some of Germany's most spectacular scenery and, unsurprisingly, doubles as a doctor's prescription to convalesce from the rigors of urbanmania. Imagine pine forests, quaint Bavarian farmhouses, onion-domed chapels, and mountain rivulets cutting through velvety meadows home to lethargic cows playing tunes with the bells hanging from their necks. Picture a meandering road, hikers carrying ornamented sticks, men clad in lederhosen, women wearing dirndls, and girls in pigtails seemingly within arm's reach of jagged peaks belonging to majestic moun-

tains. It's authentic Bavaria, the real deal, and waiting for your visit. The non-smoking Leyererhof (pictured with milk containers out front) is immaculate, and ideal for a rustic sabbatical. Michael and Martina Votz, the cordial hosts, only have seven rooms available—mainly doubles with a balcony and two apartments (but one is without a balcony)—that are often fully booked. Reserve well in advance for the summer months. Guests here are typically regulars, or friends of regulars, who stay a week or two at a time. **PRICE** (includes breakfast), 20-31€ per person per day, depending on room-type, season, and how many nights you stay. **To get there**, GPS: N47 37.725 E12 52.554, the Leyererhof is 10 km from Berchtesgaden on route 305 near the village of Ramsau (see Excursions page 15), where you'll discover one of Germany's most photographed Baroque churches. Route 305, or more famously the Deutsche Alpenstrasse (German Alpine Road), is the most scenic in the land. **Railers**, alas, there is no public transportation to this alpine neighborhood, essentially cutting you off. However, if you book at least a few nights, call ahead and they'll pick you up from Berchtesgaden's train station (but then you're on your own by foot). **Drivers, from** Berchtesgaden, take the main road (route 305) direction Ramsau and stay on this road all the way. Continue past Ramsau and climb route 305 up the hill. At the top, the road levels and your pastoral digs will eventually appear on the right. **Drivers, from** the Munich-Salzburg autobahn (A8), exit at Siegsdorf/Inzell. Follow signs to Inzell, then Berchtesgaden. After Inzell the road becomes route 305, which rambles along a tremendously scenic and curvy and narrow route (that you should avoid at night! WWII buffs will be interested to know this is the same stretch of road portrayed in the television miniseries "Band of Brothers," episode 10, "Points," when the boys of Easy Company, destination Obersalzberg, try unsuccessfully with grenades and bazookas to clear huge mounds of avalanche rubble left by last-stand Nazis). Some 20 km later you'll reach your digs on the left. **Note** that the Deutsche Alpenstrasse is rife with extended-stay vacation farmhouses similar to the Leyererhof. So, if the Leyererhof is full, and you want to overnight here, you may get lucky with one of the others.

Accommodations at Obersalzberg; (because of the rather remote location of the following two properties, Railers will need to utilize a bus—but more likely a taxi—up and down the mountain).

$$$$ **Hotel InterContinental,** (Hintereck 1, Berchtesgaden, <u>GPS</u>: N47 37.951 E13 02.796, www.ihg.com, tel. 08652/97550, toll-free reservations from USA/Canada 1-888-424-6835 or within Europe 00800-1800-1800, **free Internet**). In July 2005, the InterContinental Hotels Group (IHG) completed construction on this 138-room 5-star resort hotel on the hilltop site where Field Marshal Hermann Göring (commander of Hitler's Luftwaffe, or air force) formerly lived with his wife in their pastoral home. Wrapped in a panorama of alpine vistas, this exclusive 3-floor twin-building resort affords its guests contemporary rooms and suites with free non-alcoholic mini bar, king-sized beds, a wellness spa and fitness center, connecting indoor and outdoor heated swimming pools, banquet and conference rooms, two fine restaurants, and a traditional-style Stube drawing fresh beer from the Hofbräuhaus Berchtesgaden. **Note:** Check-in from 15:00, check-out by 12:00. Room rates vary according to season and/or advance online booking. Higher the floor the better view. If you're planning on staying a few nights, sign up for Ambassador Status on the IHG website and receive a guaranteed room upgrade (that could easily pay for the membership fee depending on your length of stay and roomtype). **PRICE**, (breakfast typically not included), Standard from 195€, Executive from 245€ (option with fireplace), Panorama Suite from 410€, Penthouse Suite from 575€. All major CCs accepted. **Drivers**, (valet) parking 15€ or park free in the lot below the hotel.

$$$ **Hotel zum Türken,** (tel. 08652/2428, open May-October otherwise closed, www.hotel-zum-tuerken.com, <u>GPS</u>: N47 38.028 E13 02.638, **no Internet** access), is one of a few original buildings left on Obersalzberg and not surprisingly a matchless overnight experience, run by Frau Monika Scharfenberg-Betzien (who continues the tradition from her late mother Ingrid Scharfenberg). As a former command center for the Reich's Security Service, located directly above the site of Hitler's Berghof (his former residence), the Türken is steeped in history and a treat for World War II buffs! Like a living museum, a time capsule of enormity, the hotel recalls the '40s and '50s with its classic paintings and furnishings, and below ground is a captivating bunker system in which I

have written a do-it-yourself tour for you. After a full day of sightseeing, reward yourself with a drink from the "honor" bar in the shared living room (take what you please and jot down your room number). Mingle with like-minded guests; (since evenings on Obersalzberg are quiet, many of the hotel guests congregate here). Although more money, reserve a front-facing room (preferably with balcony) for unforgettable views over the former Berghof site and beyond to Austria. **PRICE** (includes breakfast), Sgl 45-60€ (with shower-toilet in room 80-90€), Dbl 90-110€ (with shower-toilet in room 130-160€), extra bed 40€. **Note:** As mentioned above, reserve a front-facing room. Arrive before 18:00, when reception closes. If you don't have wheels, know that the buses to/fro Berchtesgaden stop running around 17:15 (till 18:15 Mon-Fri) and a taxi will cost roughly 13€ one way. For more history on the property and the DIY tour, see World War II Bunker page 31.

Obersalzberg
(Upper Salt Mountain)

Elevation: 970 m (3,181 ft). **Population:** A rare few.

Parked high above Berchtesgaden, Obersalzberg before 1933 was a peaceful alpine farming community sprinkled with a few summer villas and desirable vacation retreats boasting breathtaking views into Salzburg, Austria. Adolf Hitler decided this was the idyllic spot on the doorstep of his native land to call home. Dietrich Eckart—a literary connoisseur and poet, a coarse individual who drank to stay sober, a raging anti-Semite, and Hitler's mentor—introduced young Adolf to this heavenly locale in the early 1920s.

When Hitler's heavy-handed tactics won his party, the National Socialist German Workers' Party, or Nazis, enough votes in the Reichstag (parliament) to seize power in 1933, Obersalzberg lost its innocence forever.

During the mid-'30s, Martin Bormann, Hitler's personal secretary and right-hand man, kicked out the locals on Obersalzberg—many of whom belonged to families with generations of history on the mountain—and transformed their alpine oasis into a massive construction site housing upwards of 6,000 workers in temporary barracks. Albert Speer, in his book *Inside the Third Reich, Memoirs* (p. 101 in my 1970 hardcover edition), wrote of Bormann on Obersalzberg: "With total insensitivity to the natural surroundings, Bormann laid out a network of roads through this magnificent landscape. He turned forest paths, hitherto carpeted by pine needles and penetrated by roots, into paved promenades … trucks loaded with building materials rumbled along roads. At night the various building sites glowed with light, for work went on in two shifts, and occasionally detonations thundered through the valley."

Bormann was responsible for every building project in the region, including the Eagle's Nest on Mount Kehlstein. His grand plan was to create a restful neighborhood for his boss that doubled as a Nazi command center. In doing this, Bormann separated Obersalzberg into three security zones by implementing a nine-foot-high barbed-wire fence patrolled by armed guards. Albert Speer, from his aforementioned book (p. 100), likened the Führer Gebiet (Hitler's main security zone) to an "open-air enclosure for wild animals."

By means of coercion, confiscation and forced sales of properties, Bormann ultimately acquired all land from the entry road connecting Berchtesgaden with Obersalzberg to the top of Mount Kehlstein, which completed the first of around a dozen FHQs (Führerhauptquartier, or Hitler's headquarters, the most famous of which are Obersalzberg, Wolf's Lair, and the Berlin bunker).

In 1945, Allied military intelligence widely believed Hitler would quit Berlin for Obersalzberg to set up the so-called Alpine Redoubt and continue the war from the mountains. Therefore, on April 25, the Allies dialed up a massive air raid in which some 300 British Lancaster bombers sent their regards from the King and royally plastered Obersalzberg. Little more than a week later, on May 4, American military units swept through Berchtesgaden and liberated the mountain. With the exception of a few buildings, the Bavarian government razed all remnants of Hitler's Reich on Obersalzberg in 1952.

Since Obersalzberg played a major role during World War II, this chapter has been widely extended and divided into four sections: **Obersalzberg Today** (below), **Obersalzberg 1933-45** (page 22), **World War II Bunker** (page 31), and **Eagle's Nest** (page 35).

OBERSALZBERG
Today

The main reason tourists climb the narrow, curvy road from Berchtesgaden in the valley to Obersalzberg at 3,000 feet is the opportunity to hop on a specially modified bus and climb even higher to behold gargantuan views from the mountain-top Eagle's Nest. Obersalzberg, a former community at the center of an evil empire, has been virtually wiped clean except for a few haunting ghosts and Third Reich relics from Germany's dark past. Other than freshly paved parking lots, a motor pool of buses, the new Documentation Center and InterContinental resort hotel, there are few contemporary attractions to note.

The Eagle's Nest bus departure area and Documentation Center are only a short walk apart. To reach the other sites (zoo, hotels IC and Türken), walk the scenic trail behind the Documentation Center or Drivers

who plan on visiting the Türken's bunker can park in its lot.

Railers/Drivers, for detailed directions and parking, see page 37 "Getting to Obersalzberg."

Hotel InterContinental, see page 19.

World War II Bunker, see pages 25 and 31.

Eagle's Nest, page 35.

Documentation Center, (April-Oct daily 9:00-17:00 last entry 16:00, Nov-March Tue-Sun 10:00-15:00 last entry 14:00, closed Nov 1 and Jan 1 as well as Dec 24-25 and 31, adult 3€ or 2.50€ with overnight guest card, school-aged children are free as well as teachers and college students and active-duty soldiers with ID, rent the 2€ audio guide because exhibit is in German, allow 90 min to 3 hrs for a visit, **toilets** downstairs on way to bunker, www.obersalzberg.de). Set in Martin Bormann's former administration office and VIP guest house, the Documentation Center is a worthwhile exhibition combining the history of Obersalzberg with the central manifestations of the National Socialist dictatorship, the rise and fall of the Third Reich, and admission into a cavernous but humdrum section of the Obersalzberg bunker system. **To get there,** <u>GPS</u>: N47 37.812 E13 02.414, see page 37 "Getting to Obersalzberg." **Note:** The wooded path behind the property leads to Hitler's former estate within 3 minutes (descend path following the directional sign to Berchtesgaden).

Zoo, (hours tend to vary but generally May-Oct 10:00-12:00 & 13:00-16:00, closed during bad weather and Nov-April, free entry but a small donation is encouraged to help feed the animals). Privately run by an animal-loving local, this small wildlife enclosure has been a hit with big and little kids alike for decades. In general, the sanctuary accommodates turtles, owls, snakes, fish, marmots, and a few birds of prey. **To get there,** <u>GPS</u>: N47 37.967 E13 02.849, walk past the private apartments (white building) beneath the Hotel InterContinental following the wooden signs: Adler + Gehege & Greifvogelstation.

OBERSALZBERG 1933-45

After Hitler assumed power in 1933, Obersalzberg went from small-town obscurity to front-page headlines. With uncompromising resolve, Martin Bormann reshaped the Upper Salt Mountain into a center for Nazi Southern Command. Ultimately, it was all for naught—the command center was pasted by bombs and Bormann met his maker courtesy of a Soviet rendezvous on a Berlin street in May 1945. The following list of entries help recount the way it was at Obersalzberg during the days of the Third Reich. To orient yourself, refer to the hand-drawn map on page 24. **Railers,** see page 37 "Getting to Obersalzberg." Note: To walk past all of the following sites would take a few hours and is therefore only recommended for buffs. Non-buffs should focus on the Eagle's Nest, VIP Guest House, and the Hotel Türken with its intriguing bunker system (which I have written a self-guided tour for you on page 32). **Drivers,** entries are listed in the order they will be reached when coming from central Berchtesgaden; (see page 37 "Getting to Obersalzberg"). Tips and suggestions are offered along the way. Read ahead, and be prepared for sites that are either hard to find or nonexistent.

☞   Drivers, at the turn off from Berchtesgaden (bridge over river), pass the first of several former guard posts up to Obersalzberg. The road (route 319) from here climbs at a demanding pace; after about 2.5 km you'll reach the green "Obersalzberg" sign—beyond it (right) is the road (Antenbergweg) that led up to Speer's former house and studio.

Haus Speer, (rusted copper-green roof in background, briefly seen from road; you'll have a much better view of both Haus and Studio Speer when coming back down the hill). Albert Speer was Hitler's favorite architect, who joined the Nazi party in 1931 as member No. 474,481. Hitler was so impressed by Speer's charisma and architectural flair that he rewarded him with his grand plan to reconstruct Berlin into Germania (never completed), capital of Nazi-occupied Europe. Other monumental projects awarded to Speer were the Reich's Chancellery in Berlin, and the Rally Grounds in Nürnberg, including the fanatically celebrated 1934 party convention at Zeppelin Field. After the sudden death of Fritz Todt in 1942 (plane crash over Russia), Speer was appointed his ministerial position of overseeing "armaments and war production." This gained Speer exclusive access to the Führer, further bonding their unique relationship. Consequently, Speer had to be available at a moment's notice and was therefore furnished with this modest chalet-style house. **Today**, the former Speer property is privately owned and not open to visitors.

After the war, during the 1946 Nürnberg trials, Speer was sentenced to 20 years in Spandau prison, Berlin. While reflecting on his relationship with Hitler, Speer declared: "One seldom recognizes the devil when he puts his hand on your shoulder." Albert Speer died in 1981 and is buried in the Bergfriedhof, Heidelberg.

Studio Speer, (red terracotta-tiled roof in foreground). Speer, including Adolf Hitler, spent many hours in this roadside studio mulling over architectural models, intricate drawings and grandiose projects-to-be. After the war, Speer's studio was converted into the Evergreen Lodge, suite-style accommodations belonging to the AFRC (Armed Forces Recreational Center) General Walker resort (closed 1995). **Today**, both former Speer properties are privately owned and off-limits to passersby (like you and me).

Gutshof & Pig Stables, (accessible via road on left, opposite road climbing to Haus Speer). Bormann constructed the Gutshof and pig stables to serve as a model Nazi farm. His concept, however, didn't exactly outshine any *real* farm because bumptious Bormann evicted the local farmers in 1933—and generals, including politicians, don't make good farmers! Instead, the Gutshof became more of a hobby for Bormann to keep Haflinger mountain ponies and colonies of bees producing sweet honey. After the war, the Gutshof was converted into the Skytop Lodge as part of the AFRC (Armed Forces Recreational Center) General Walker resort (closed 1995) and primarily used as a ski school in winter and a golf course in summer. **Today**, it still serves as a clubhouse for the 9-hole golf course, including a restaurant. Nothing remains of the pig stables.

☞   Drivers, continue up the road and at the junction (on right curve) go straight (direction Hotel Türken)—this was the entrance to Adolf-Hitler-Strasse, where another SS guard post was positioned (foundations remain). Look left and (if its cloudless) a distant view to the fortress of Salzburg will briefly emerge. On the knoll to the right is where Hitler lived in his three-story mansion, the Berghof. The beginning section of his driveway will appear shortly on the right. Ahead on the hill is the Hotel Türken, where you'll find the World War II Bunker (Bunkeranlagen) page 31.

Haus Hitler, (aka the Berghof, <u>GPS</u>: N47 38.040 E13 02.553). In 1927, Hitler moved into Haus Wachenfeld, an unpretentious chalet. By 1936, Haus Wachenfeld had received a monstrous overhaul deserving of the nation's chancellor. Hitler designed the new look himself, transforming the chalet into the so-called Berghof, a three-story mansion with more than 30 rooms. The Berghof's architectural highlight was an enormous picture-frame window (4m x 8m/13ft x 26ft) in the living room that could be hydraulically lowered into the windowsill adding a natural, airy quality to an already awesome view into Austria. Albert Speer, in his book *Inside the Third Reich, Memoirs* (p. 102 in my 1970 hardcover edition), commented on how Hitler's design of the Berghof was substandard and if a professor had to evaluate the work (without the threat of being shot) he probably would have given it a D grade. Speer used the picture-frame window as the prime example in his assessment, saying Hitler curiously designed the massive window above the garage, which "when the wind was unfavorable, a strong smell of gasoline penetrated into the living room."

OBERSBG. 1933-45

Before the war, the Berghof became an alternative center of government, where Hitler held important meetings rather than in Berlin or Munich. Prominent visitors included Benito Mussolini ("Il Duce"), British Prime Minister Neville Chamberlain, Britain's Foreign Minister Lord Halifax, King Boris of Bulgaria, and even the Duke (Edward) and Duchess (Simpson) of Windsor (who caused a storm of controversy in 1936 when King Edward VIII chose to abdicate the British throne to marry Wallis Simpson, a twice-divorced American. Subsequently, Edward received the title of duke. The public had their doubts whether or not they were Nazi sympathizers. Edward abdicated the throne to his brother George VI, whose royal stammer was the subject of the Academy Award winning film "The King's Speech").

As the war progressed and the incessant aerial bombardment of German cities became a harsh reality, Hitler retreated to the Berghof not for a holiday but to hide from the grim reality of Germany's future. Hitler would leave Obersalzberg and his beloved Berghof for the last time on July 14, 1944, when he departed for his headquarters at the so-called Wolf's Lair by Rastenburg, East Prussia (today's Ketrzyn, Poland). In the end, the Berghof was blasted by a storm of bombs on April 25, 1945, and **today** the only parts remaining are the beginning section of driveway and back retaining wall.

Hotel Türken, (GPS: N47 38.028 E13 02.638). The age-old Hotel Türken did not fall prey to Bormann's bulldozers but instead it was virtually stolen from its owners by the Reich's Security Service (Reichssicherheitsdienst)—being next door to Hitler's Berghof, it was too convenient a location. When you visit, notice the one-man guard post out front by the street. For more on the Hotel Türken and its bunker, read the next entry then flip to the next section, World War II Bunker (page 31).

Bunker System, locally Bunkeranlagen. It is easy to understand in the beginning of the war why terms such as "air raid" or "underground shelter" were taboo in Hitler's peaceful neighborhood. By the middle of 1943, however, the Allies increased the air war over Germany to daily sorties and the Nazi war machine had suffered great defeats on the Eastern front, e.g. Stalingrad and Kursk. Hitler had no choice but to agree on a new construction project for his alpine command center. Engineers scrambled to devise plans, which were drafted, evaluated, modified, disapproved, redrafted, and finally approved to relocate Nazi Southern Command underground for a possible last stand. By war's end, the bunker system (or network of air-raid shelters) was estimated to be 5 km (3 mi) long. All tunnels were interlinked, except Herman Göring's bunker with Martin Bormann's because of an internal rivalry.

As for the construction of the tunnels, you'll have to imagine thousands of craftsmen and laborers rotating shifts every eight hours, working in overly cramped conditions. While a mason cemented the ceiling of an entrance, for example, plumbers, electricians and handymen had to crawl between his legs to get to their positions. The excavated dirt was trucked miles away to elude detection via aerial reconnaissance. **Note:** For a do-it-yourself subterranean adventure, flip to World War II Bunker page 31.

Haus Bormann, (formerly located on the hillside across the road from the Hotel Türken). Martin Bormann lived in a large, two-story house that externally appeared rustic Bavarian while internally it was outfitted with state-of-the-art amenities and luxurious furnishings, even the children's rooms were fit for royalty. Bormann acquired the property from Dr. Seitz, who locally ran a children's medical clinic. The acquisition was meticulously planned. Since it overlooked the Berghof, he could observe Hitler's every move. Bormann had the unusual ability to influence Hitler when others couldn't. As a result of Bormann's tireless energy and obsessive nature to serve his master, he was always informed of Hitler's state of affairs, and even on matters that were none of his business. He frequently traveled with Hitler while his wife and nine children lived here permanently at Obersalzberg. It was during these times that Mrs. Bormann, the children, and Eva Braun regularly made use of the Eagle's Nest—the mountaintop perch that Bormann insisted on building for his boss, whom he must have known had a fear of heights! According to James P. O'Donnell in his book, *The Bunker* (p. 300-306 in my 2001 paperback edition), Bormann died on the streets of Berlin at approximately 3:30 a.m. May 2, 1945, following Hitler's suicide and the "breakout." **Today**, nothing remains of Haus Bormann and trees have overgrown the site.

Kindergarten, Archives & Admin: Situated directly above the Hotel Türken, the administration building belonged to the SS barracks (see next entry). Adjacent were the archives (a studio containing models of future projects for the neighborhood) and the kindergarten for the children of Obersalzberg personnel. **Today**, nothing remains of these structures.

SS Barracks: To bolster Hitler's security, barracks for a battalion of black-uni-formed SS (Schutz Staffel or protection guard) and elite Leibstandarte troops were constructed near his house. These consisted of residence quarters, a motor pool, mess hall, and (to ensure continued tranquility on Obersalzberg) an underground rifle range.

In 1952, the barracks were razed and later landscaped into a soccer field. *More than a decade ago, in preparation for the new Eagle's Nest bus departure area, the soccer field was redeveloped. During this project much of the past was unearthed, such as unused ammunition, movie reels, official Nazi documents, SS porcelain wares, bottles of wine seized during the occupation of France, and many other knickknacks needed to

sustain 600 Hugo Boss-wearing SS troops. **Today**, buses departing for the Eagle's Nest drive right through the site of the former SS barracks. *The two **pictures** were taken in the year 2001 by yours truly during the redevelopment of the SS barracks site for the present-day Eagle's Nest bus departure area. In the picture above you can see the construction site adjacent to the original bus departure area. The line of trees in the background shield the former locations of the greenhouse, air-raid warning center, and Haus Göring (presently the site of the Hotel InterContinental). The second picture shows the construction site with Untersberg mountain in the background.

Greenhouse: Hitler was a strict vegetarian and the greenhouse supplied ample produce for his cravings, as well as a fresh supply of flowers for the homes of high-ranking officers. What's more, the greenhouse provided the perfect location for Eva Braun and her helpers to arrange Easter-egg hunts for the officers' children. **Today**, only the back retaining wall remains and the greenhouse site is now a parking lot for employees of the Hotel InterContinental.

Air-Raid Warning Center: While Hitler and his top brass were managing the war from Obersalzberg, the air-raid warning center was on high alert. Entrenched within the hill behind the greenhouse, this cavernous bunker featured the most modern technological equipment known, which detected air traffic over Nazi-occupied Europe by relaying signals from the various radar stations positioned throughout the territories. If enemy planes were headed for Obersalzberg, the 11 antiaircraft units in the Berchtesgaden district would then be contacted and ready for action within six minutes.

Additionally, the air-raid center governed a smoke-screen department comprised of three batteries, each having more than 250 smoke-screen devices loyal to the districts of Berchtesgaden, Obersalzberg, Königssee and Bad Reichenhall. If the order was given, the entire district could be blanketed by smoke within 30 minutes, making it virtually impossible for the enemy to achieve a successful bombing run.

But what made the British bombing raid on Wednesday, April 25, 1945, such a success was by this late stage in the war the Germans had lost so much territory that the bombers flew most of their mission over friendly terrain. By the time functioning German radar stations actually picked up the signal of approaching enemy aircraft, the bombers were only some 60 km (37 mi) away. Thus, Hitler's neighborhood and command center were blown to smithereens without the bombers being subjected to much antiair-craft fire. **Today**, nothing remains of the air-raid warning center (it was uprooted along with the remains of Haus Göring during construction of the Hotel InterContinental).

Haus Göring; (the new Hotel InterContinental sits on top of the Haus Göring site). Born south of Munich in the rosy town of Rosenheim, Hermann Göring was a full-blooded Bavarian who treasured his family's deep-rooted heritage. He often donned tailor-made lederhosen, went deer hunting with pals, and drank beer by the liter. Göring became a hero to most Germans during World War I as a flamboyant and successful fight-er pilot. In 1918, upon the death of Germany's internationally famed ace of aces, Manfred von Richthofen (better known as the Red Baron), Göring was honored with the command of Richthofen's legendary fighter group, Jagdgeschwader 1, a.k.a. the Flying Circus.

In the early 1920s, Hitler met Göring through his writer friend Dietrich Eckart. As a struggling politician, Hitler rode the social wave of Göring's celebrity. Germany's chancellor-to-be and the WWI hero teamed up as partners with a purpose, attending nu-merous public rallies and private functions together. As one of the original Nazis, Göring participated in the 1923 Beer Hall Putsch. During the latter failed coup, Göring was seri-ously wounded thus he fled the country until an amnesty allowed him to return in 1927.

Years later, during the Third Reich, Hitler awarded the narcissistic Göring many titles, such as police chief of Prussia; original head of the Gestapo (Secret State Police); commander of the Luftwaffe (German air force); and, ultimately, Göring was given the bejeweled baton that came with the elite title of Herr Reichsmarschall (Field Marshal).

When Göring moved to Obersalzberg he had a traditional Bavarian-style house built with a Hollywoodesque swimming pool landscaped into the front yard. Göring owned the estate for a decade before fleeing Germany at the end of the war. He was eventually picked up in Austria by U.S. troops and subsequently sentenced to death by hanging at the Nürnberg trials. Hours before his scheduled execution on October 15, 1946, Göring cheated the hangman by swallowing a hidden capsule of poison.

The foundations of Göring's house, along with the cellar and front-yard pool, re-mained somewhat intact right up until the turn of the new millennium (circa 2001), when work began on the 138-room InterContinental resort hotel (page 19).

Göring's Adjutant: In the neighboring white-washed apartment building lived General Bodenschatz, Göring's chief of staff, as well as a few other officers and their families. **Today**, the building still serves as apartments, seven in fact, and you'll walk by them if you visit the zoo.

Coal Bunker, (GPS: N47 37.934 E13 02.918). Not far away, a huge concrete edifice was constructed to store tons of coal for the assorted needs of Obersalzberg personnel. Trucks would fill the internal storage units by unloading their cargo into the top of the structure via the above access road. **Today**, the coal bunker is kaput but largely intact.

Mooslahnerkopf: When Hitler was in residence at Obersalzberg and managing Nazi Southern Command, he made it part of his daily routine with favorable weather to take an afternoon stroll to his preferred tea house. Not the mountaintop Eagle's Nest, since Hitler had a fear of heights, but the Teehaus at the Mooslahnnerkopf hill and lookout. The walk there, flanked by tall evergreen trees and deli-cate alpine flora, was a time of peace for a man at war with the world. It was here at the Mooslahnnerkopf that Hitler enjoyed the company of his guests over cof-fee and cake and he walked his dog Blondie while con-

OBERSBG. 1933-45

versing with generals and admiring the sweeping vistas into Austria from the wooden

railing wrapped around the horseshoe-shaped lookout. **Today**, the lookout (pictured) remains virtually the same with stunning views reaching as far as the fortress of Salzburg. (The railing, however, has since been replaced with a near replica.) On the other hand, the tea house was completely razed in 2006. All that remains to mark its former location is a rock wall with a graffiti'd tea cup (pictured).

Albert Speer, in his book *Inside the Third Reich, Memoirs* (p. 106-107 in my 1970 hardcover edition), described a typical afternoon at the Teehaus with Hitler and his guests: "Shortly after dinner the walk to the teahouse began. The width of the path left room for only two abreast, so that the file resembled a procession. Two security men walked at the head. Then came Hitler with one other person, with whom he conversed, followed in any order by the dinner company, with more guards bringing up the rear. Hitler's two police dogs roamed about the area and ignored his commands—the only oppositionists at his court. To Bormann's vexation, Hitler was addicted to this particular walk, which took about half an hour, and disdained using the mile-long paved forest roads.'

"The teahouse had been built at one of Hitler's favorite lookout points above the Berchtesgaden valley. The company always marveled at the panorama in the same phrases. ... The teahouse itself consisted of a round room about twenty-five feet in diameter, pleasing in its proportions, with a row of small-paned windows and a fireplace along the interior wall. The company sat in easy chairs around the round table, with Eva Braun and one of the other ladies again at Hitler's side. Those who did not find seats went into a small adjoining room. According to taste, one had tea, coffee, or chocolate, and various types of cake and cookies, followed by liqueurs. Here, at the coffee table, Hitler was particularly fond of drifting into endless monologues. The subjects were mostly familiar to the company, who therefore listened absently, though pretending attention. Occasionally Hitler himself fell asleep over one of his monologues. The company then continued chatting in whispers, hoping that he would awaken in time for the evening meal. It was all very familial. ... After about two hours the teatime ended, generally around six."

To get there, the Mooslanhnerkopf site and lookout is well worth the 20-min walk (each way) if you have the time (allow an hour with sightseeing). The starting point is the graveled footpath leading into the woods across from the Hotel Türken. (Drivers, consider doing my DIY bunker tour first, pages 31-34, then leave your car in the lot, otherwise park elsewhere and walk back, e.g. by the Documentation Center, which is also easy.) Continue on the graveled footpath a short distance and prior to the sweeping left curve take the shortcut on the right through the shrubbery and down the man-made steps to intersect the path. Continue downhill on this abundantly scenic track as it meanders along the golf course like a conveyer belt past majestic mountains and through pinewood forests while the sound of distant cowbells complement the alpine air. At the golf green and tee, descend the path a short distance farther as it bends right then cut *left on the trail heading into the woods and shrubbery. (*If you start sharply downhill, you missed the left turn. Always keep the golf course to your left.) The trail (that was very muddy

when I visited) will soon widen. Stay on this path all the way to the Mooslanhnerkopf at the end, where you'll reach the lookout and tea house site. (Pictured is yours truly sitting on the bench at the lookout and marveling the beauty of Berchtesgadenerland.)

☞ Drivers, when ready, turn around and head back past the Hotel Türken and Hitler's

former estate to the junction, turn left (direction Obersalzberg) and climb the windy road to the next sites. To the right of the last curve, marked by a graveled pull-over area and a yellow directional sign, begins the footpath to the theater ruins. Continue a short distance farther up the hill and on the right you'll see a power station (pictured). Behind it are vestiges of the Kampfhäusl. Park in the lot opposite, or where convenient, and return here on foot. The remaining sites are only meters away, with the exception of Haus Eckart.

Kampfhäusl: Hitler moved into this petite log cabin after serving a 13-month jail sentence at Landsberg prison (Nov 1923—Dec '24). It was here that in 1925 he wrote the second and final part of his political manifesto, "Mein Kampf" (My Struggle). In 1927, he moved a few properties over to Haus Wachenfeld, which later morphed into the Berghof mansion and the nucleus

of Nazi Southern Command. **Today**, vestiges of the structure's stone foundation still remain (pictured). To find it, step behind the power station and follow the trail right. A short distance ahead on the left, climb the hillside to the remains of the Kampfhäusl.

Theater: Helping to maintain high morale of the military personnel at Obersalzberg, a 2,000-seat theater hall was constructed to present the latest films and German stage productions, as well as propaganda newsreels from the front. Hitler seldom visited. During the April 1945 air raid the theater collapsed, but **today** some of the enormous concrete support pylons still remain. **To get there**, at the gravel pull-over area, begin hiking the trail. It will veer right and flatten out—(do not take the path that continues to climb)—follow this straight (direction Berchtesgaden) to the ruins, 3 min.

VIP Guest House: Originally part of Pension Moritz (explained in next entry), the cottage was acquired by Martin Bormann and renovated into his administration office in addition to a VIP guest house to accommodate the businessmen with whom he had dealings. **Today**, the structure is the Documentation Center (page 21). **Note** that the graveled path descending through the woods behind the property leads to Hitler's former estate in about 3 minutes (follow directional sign to Berchtesgaden).

Volkshotel Platterhof: Obersalzberg tourism began right here in the 19th century when a visionary named Mauritia Mayer, called Moritz by her friends, bought a ranch and developed the property into Pension Moritz. Profiting from Obersalzberg's clean air, Mayer marketed her pension as a healthy vacation. The rich and famous took to the idea and filled the rooms. Distinguished guests included Sigmund Freud, Johannes Brahms, and members of the Bavarian, Prussian and Austrian ruling families. Pension Moritz even attracted Dietrich Eckart, who in turn brought his protégé, Adolf Hitler.

In the 1930s, Hitler's regime acquired the pension and renovated it into the fashionable 150-bed Volkshotel (People's Hotel) Platterhof. Initially, for 1 Reich's mark per night, roughly U.S. 33¢, party members could book a room to be near their beloved Führer. The deal, however, was soon upgraded to indulge only bigwigs, when in 1937 even they were not allowed on the mountain, except by special invitation.

After the war, the U.S. repaired the damage from the April 25 bombing raid and the former Nazi hotel reopened as an AFRC resort (Armed Forces Recreation Center) under the moniker "General Walker." For more than 40 years the General Walker was a bustling

resort hotel for American soldiers and their families  until the U.S. government closed its doors in 1995 (as a result of military downsizing) and returned the property to the German government. **In conclusion**, the esteemed 19th-century Pension Moritz was converted to a swanky Nazi hotel that got bombed by the British, rebuilt by the Americans, and *razed by the Germans to become a revenue-making parking lot in the 21st century (3€ per automobile). *The picture, taken in the year 2000, shows the General Walker meeting its fate with the wrecking ball.

Post Office: Across from the Platterhof was a general store and post office for the convenience of Obersalzberg personnel. **Today**, the former post-office site is a traffic circle and mini parking area.

Haus Eckart: Dietrich Eckart often found himself in trouble with the law and would therefore go into hiding at this isolated residence parked on a scenic slope 6 km south of Obersalzberg. Eckart died in 1923 shortly after the failure of the Beer Hall Putsch and is buried in Berchtesgaden's oldest cemetery (page 11) in company with Mauritia "Moritz" Mayer (1833-97). In 1942, the Nazis made the "Eckarthaus" an annex to the Volkshotel Platterhof. After the war, Eckart's picturesque property was acquired by the U.S. military and subsequently renamed the Hinterbrand Lodge for use as a recreational resort. From 1971 to 2003 the property was employed by DoDDS-E (Department of Defense Dependents Schools-Europe) as an education facility. **Today**, the Hinterbrand Lodge is once again administered by the U.S. Army as a retreat for its personnel.

☞   **That's a wrap, folks!** I hope your explorations were gratifying, even serendipitous. I'll see you later in the World War II Bunker (below), and on the bus up to the Eagle's Nest (page 35).

OBERSBG. 1933-45

WORLD WAR II
BUNKER

👆 (This bunker is located beneath the Hotel zum Türken. To fully understand its origin, I have outlined a basic history.)

Our story begins in the 17th century with a soldier's return from fighting the Turkish siege of Vienna in 1683. The Turks lost the battle and the allies who fought to defend the Austrian capital came home triumphant. Upon the green alpine pastures of Obersalzberg the celebrated veteran built himself a homestead that became known as "zum Türken," or To the Turk.

Two centuries later, Herr Schuster, an innkeeper, bought the Türken with his wife in 1911 and rebuilt the significant hotel property we see today. Together with the nearby Platterhof Inn (previously Pension Moritz), Hotel zum Türken entertained prominent members of the royal family and celebrities of the era.

In the early 1930s, the area around the Türken buzzed with optimistic nationals shunning the Great Depression. The previous decade had been much worse for the German people, who had seen their currency massively devalued to billions, 40 percent unemployment, and scandalous politics. The time was ripe for a new beginning. Germany's savior was seemingly Herr Schuster's new neighbor, Adolf Hitler.

In January 1933, Hitler was elected chancellor of Germany and within a month he enabled parliament (on account of the Reichstag fire) to sanction him with special powers comparable to absolute dictatorship. At this time, the Nazis, Hitler's party, insisted on buying the Türken. However, Herr Schuster's answer was blunt: 'Tell Herr Hitler, I will not sell.'

Schuster, an opponent of National Socialism, did not agree with the brash ways of his new neighbor and did the unthinkable: He publicly spoke his mind. The brown shirts, Hitler's army of thugs, consequently arrested Schuster after orchestrating a boycott of the Türken to ward off any possible commerce. Nazi signs placed outside the property warned potential customers that 'A good German would never do business with a traitor'! Schuster's new address was Dachau, an internment camp for enemies of the state.

The Schuster family was subsequently exiled from Berchtesgaden. They fled 50 km north to Seebruck, an idyllic town on the Bavarian blue waters of Lake Chiemsee. Herr Schuster was released from Dachau a month later. He never fully recovered from the ensuing traumas and died the following year at age 56, but not before the Nazis forced him to sell the Türken for a fraction of its value.

The Nazis requisitioned the Türken for the service of the Reichssicherheitsdienst (RSD, or Reich's Security Service) under Heinrich Himmler, head of Nazi police forces. Being situated above the Berghof, Hitler's home, the Türken provided the perfect outpost from which to safeguard the chancellor. As the war progressed, a tunnel system was excavated beneath the Türken that ran directly under the Berghof. Loaded with specially trained SS guards and laced with deadly machine-gun nests, Hitler could have retreated here for a last stand.

The tunnel system at the Türken provides us with the unique opportunity to delve into a World War II bunker—an underground labyrinth leading into the incandescent world of a past era. Come on, let's go and have a peek.

(**To reach the Hotel Türken** on foot from the Eagle's Nest bus departure area or the "Dokumentation" bus stop, head to the Documentation Center and behind it walk the wooded path [following the directional sign to Berchtesgaden] to Hitler's former estate in about 3 minutes. Continue up the road to the Türken.)

Bunker, <u>GPS</u>: N47 38.028 E13 02.638, open April 5 through Nov 2, 2014 Wed thru Mon (closed Tuesday!) 10:00-15:00—last entry 30 min before closing—mid-May thru mid-Oct till 17:00, admission 3.50€, child 11yr and younger free. **Note:** Within the bunker is a constant 9°C (48F). But more importantly there are a large number of stairs to negotiate, which may be taxing to some people. Aside from the bunker, the property doubles as a hotel-pension (run by Monika Scharfenberg-Betzien, who continues the tradition from her late mother Ingrid Scharfenberg who left us February 2013). After World War II, Herr Schuster's daughter (Therese Partner, the grandmother of Scharfenberg-

Betzien) was allowed to move into the bombed ruins with her daughter Ingrid and reclaim the property. In 1958, after years of gritty work rebuilding the residence, Therese was given permission to reopen **Hotel zum Türken** (page 19). **Opinion:** A trip to the bunker is worth your time; and if you're lucky you'll run into Frau Scharfenberg-Betzien, Herr Schuster's great granddaughter. **Pictured** on the previous page is the Türken today, looking much like it did before the war. Pictured here is Ingrid and me (taken in the year 2000) sitting outside the Türken. I'm holding a swing-top Hofbräu beer bottle that I had just unearthed while rummaging through the former SS barracks site. The bottle was likely discarded by construction workers in the 1930s. I saw numerous bottles that had been shattered into hundreds of pieces but only one that was completely intact and in good condition.

DO-IT-YOURSELF TOUR,
World War II Bunker

Duration 20-45 min. The amount of time you spend inside the bunker depends on whether you're in a hurry or not. Time-crunched tourists can move through pretty fast; the only slowdown will be the flights of stairs. Visitors with time will want to move at a slower pace and perhaps climb into the machine-gun nests for a gunner's perspective (explained in Step 10). With that said, let's get movin'...

Step 1) Go through the turnstile gate and begin descending the spiral staircase. A short way down (on the 16th step) turn left (toilet on left) and walk to the end. These are Gefängniszellen, or jail cells. No need to conjure harsh treatment, not much actually happened here. The so-called villains they were meant for didn't frequent Obersalzberg. If there were such criminals or conspirators, they would have most likely been found and detained by Polizei in Berchtesgaden. The real horror stories that you're familiar with, *Vee haff vays of mayking zu tawk* (pathetic impression I know), took place at Prinz-Albrecht-Strasse 8, Berlin—headquarters to the Gestapo and Heinrich Himmler. (The latter HQ is now the Topography of Terror exhibition in Berlin.)

Only recently was this section painted black to represent the soot that coated the walls from the fire that broke out as a result of the British bombing raid on April 25, 1945. (Another reason for the paint job was to conceal the incessant graffiti in these rooms left behind by vandals.)

Step 2) Continue down the spiral staircase. At the bottom is an excellent opportunity to see the way the Obersalzberg tunnels were constructed: two layers of bricks coupled with concrete, insulation, two more rows of bricks and more concrete—generally a meter thick until natural rock is reached.

Step 3) Continue forward to the junction. Left or right, which will it be? — If you were to go left, you'd come to a bricked-off dead end. This formerly connected the rest of the tunnel network, e.g. Martin Bormann's digs, administration, the kindergarten, SS barracks, and so on. — Go right to the next staircase but pay close attention to the concrete floor; the ceiling light will illuminate the "jackboot" footprints left behind by impatient German officers.

Step 4) At the top of the staircase you'll see an inscription on the wall (post war) explaining that at this point you are 10 m (33 ft) underground. Notice the concrete lids to your right; these covered the hot-air duct. The above brackets secured the water pipe. Walk down the steps to the bottom and <u>stop</u>; *don't* turn the corner.

Step 5) Look back up the stairs and imagine this: It's May 4, 1945, and your company has just secured everything above ground. The task at hand is to expel any last-stand Nazis from the bunker system. You're a private in Uncle Sam's army and the job has landed in your lap. The only way out is to weasel a pardon. "Wait! I've got a wife, and kids." But there's nothing you can do; it's your turn. You hand over your wallet to your buddy together with the farewell letter you wrote your family weeks earlier in case you cop it sweet somewhere on the battlefield.

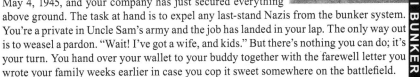

To get back to where you're standing—if there were Nazis still at their posts, our private wouldn't have made it any farther than the top of the stairs. That's because you're standing in front of a machine-gun nest. The Seh Schlitz is the peephole and the other slots are to shoot through: Schiesscharte.

Step 6) Walk the next few feet and <u>stop</u> at the top of the steps; *don't* go down them. While standing here, <u>without bending over</u>, what do you see? You see a sloping ceiling. If somehow our private had made it past the first welcoming party, then the second group of diehards would have just sliced him in two at the waist. Go down the steps and you'll be faced with another machine-gun nest.

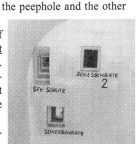

Step 7) Navigate the corridor and <u>stop</u> before the doorway; *don't* enter the next room.

Step 8) Notice the concrete frame where a watertight iron door was fitted. If our private had miraculously made it this far, he would've been trapped between the locked iron door and welcoming party number three behind him. Turn around to see yet another machine-gun position.

Step 9) Step through the doorway. Congratulations, you've just made it into Hitler's cold and clammy foyer, 70 m (230 ft) underground. From here you'll notice a few things. Let's start with what looks like another prison cell. If Hitler were to have taken up residence below ground, this cell would've been the home (kennel) for his dog, Blondie.

Above the entrance you came through you'll see a gas duct (Schleuse); these were installed throughout the bunker system to prevent the airways from being used forcibly. The writing on the wall to the right explains that construction of the Obersalzberg bunker system began mid-August 1943 and its details are described in a book for sale upstairs at the cashier.

Hitler's bodyguard, or Leibwache, occupied this area. Hence the two openings (left of bricked-off doorway) that were used as domestic facilities and a sleeping room (Schlafraum) in the back. Within the second entrance it looks like our nervous private heard some noises and let his rifle rock 'n' roll.

We see more writing to the right of the bricked-off doorway. It reads: "Behind this door were the rooms of Hitler, Eva Braun, and Dr. Morell."

Adolf had 19 rooms in his bunker and most were lavishly decorated with marble, wood paneling, tapestries, chandeliers, carpeting, and parquet floors. The equivalent of millions of dollars were spent making all this possible while the nation had to ration even the most basic foods, in addition to melting church bells, for the war effort. But it was all for naught, Hitler never stayed here!

Step 10) You have a choice of two stairways; they both lead to the same place. Face the aforementioned gas duct and descend the stairway on the right.

At the bottom of the stairs you have the opportunity (right) to *climb up and into those three machine-gun nests that we passed on the way in. It's worth the climb, even if your hands smell like rust afterwards. Bring your camera. Shoot a photo from the gunner's perspective as a private belonging to your company tries to breach the premises. (*Note: Before you begin exploring the machine-gun nests, let's first finish our tour since it's almost over.)

To the left of the staircase you'll see three things: another bricked-off wall that formerly led under Hitler's house; a cubical designated "Maschinenraum" (machine shop), which facilitated the heating, lighting and ventilation in the bunker; and you'll see a corridor—head down this to the doorway.

Step 11) At the junction you can go left or straight, either way you end up in the same place. Let's go straight—if you're with a small group, send half to the left—mind your head on the way through.

To your immediate left is the inside of another gunner's position. A few feet farther and you'll be inside yet another nest; here you can witness the ramifications of repeated bazooka blasts by our jumpy private and his comrades. This provides a unique opportunity to see firsthand how the Nazis reinforced their fortifications, such as the Atlantic Wall. The barred passage led out the side of the mountain—depending on the situation, this could have been utilized as a secret entrance or an escape route.

That's a wrap, folks! I hope you enjoyed yourself and continue to do so. Take your time and remember…all paths lead up, and out.

And to conclude the final entry in the journal of our brave private: He never encountered any resistance in the bunker that afternoon, surviving to once again enjoy the wonder of life that many of us take for granted everyday. Then why the bazooka blasts? Why the heck not. The war in Europe was over!

WWII BUNKER

EAGLE'S NEST

Elevation: 1,834 m (6,017 ft).

The Eagle's Nest, locally known as the "Kehlsteinhaus," is a petite yet solid structure built from massive granite blocks cemented into the summit of Mount Kehlstein at 6,017 feet. The views are stunning from its perch and the road leading up the mountain is also something to marvel. From Obersalzberg at 3,100 feet the road steeply climbs four miles up the mountain face to the entrance of a 400-foot tunnel blasted into the dense rock, where visitors walk the remaining leg to Hitler's former elevator that lifts its occupants 400 feet within 45 seconds into the heart of the Eagle's Nest.

In just 13 months 3,500 workers from 1937-38 completed the entire Eagle's Nest project: access roads, tunneling, elevator, and the structure itself. To facilitate such swift results the mountainside was illuminated throughout the night allowing construction to

continue nonstop. While several work crews were forging the road, others were simultaneously building the Nest with the aid of a cable-car system hauling up materials. Even by today's standards the Eagle's Nest project is seen as a remarkable feat of engineering.

It is stated that Hitler was given the Eagle's Nest by the party as a present on his 50th birthday, but surely someone must have known Hitler had a fear of heights and a touch of claustrophobia; (the elevator on the way up can be a bit unsettling). Needless to say, the goofy-mustached tyrant wasn't a great admirer of the property, officially visiting it 14 times between September 1938 and October 1940. Unofficially, there are only a handful of visits noted. The biggest function held at the Nest was a wedding reception in June '44—the guests of honor were Eva Braun's sister, Gretl, and SS General Herman Fegelein. Hitler did not attend. A year later, Hitler had Fegelein killed in Berlin. But that's another story.

To dispel the myth, there are no bedrooms in the Eagle's Nest and Hitler never spent the night. There were, however, a few bunk beds situated in the cellar for guards stationed on the premises; (today the cellar is off limits to visitors).

Fortunately, during the immense bombing raid on April 25, 1945, the British missed the Eagle's Nest and it therefore remains in original condition. Today, around 300,000 tourists per year (May-Oct) visit the mountaintop chalet, which is managed by the Berchtesgadener Land Tourism Office and marketed as a scenic restaurant.

Hours: The Eagle's Nest is open daily from mid-May thru October, depending on weather. It is closed the rest of the year due to mammoth amounts of snow.

Price (includes round-trip bus fare from Obersalzberg to the Eagle's Nest and entry into the structure), adult 16.10€, youth 6-14yr 9.30€, family 35€ (or 22€ for single parent with child). CC: VC, MC. Purchase your ticket from the cashier prior to boarding at the Eagle's Nest bus departure area, Obersalzberg. **Note:** No student or senior discount is available but holders of the overnight guest card will receive 1.50€ off admission.

Toilets at the bus departure area are just past the ticket counter and souvenir shops.

Buses to Eagle's Nest, (departing mid-May thru October). The first bus to depart Obersalzberg for the Eagle's Nest is 8:30 (15-min trip)—after this, buses depart every 25 min until the last one at 16:00 (but don't take this last bus otherwise you'll leave yourself with no time). The last bus down from the Nest departs at 16:25 (15-min trip)—don't miss this or it's a long, albeit scenic, walk back—but note that often during peak times they allocate an extra few buses down at 16:50 to manage the latecomers and overflow (if you think this may be you, ask if 16:50 is available when getting your ticket stamped with your desired return time, explained in the next entry "Note").

Note: Once the bus arrives at the Eagle's Nest, get in line at the window on the right to have your ticket stamped with your desired return time. As a heads up, the available return times are located behind the bus driver. Decide which one is best for you. Consider a departure time of at least 70 minutes after your arrival. If the weather is nice and you're a history buff, allow 90-120 min. Calculate whether you're going to eat or drink something at the restaurant. Also note that during peak times (e.g. July/Aug, sunny weather, mid-morning) a 10-15 min wait in the tunnel for the elevator is not uncommon.

Opinion: The most scenic seats on the way up to the Nest are on the right side of the bus. On the way down, I recommend you sit on the left (driver's) side of the bus (and if available sit in the very last/back row).

Suggestion: Instead of taking the elevator back down from inside the Nest, allow at least 20 min to walk to the bus area via the scenic path beginning at the side of the structure.

Tours: If you're interested in a private or group tour of the Eagle's Nest and Obersalzberg, contact **Eagle's Nest Historical Tours** (page 3). Or at last minute, i.e. without a reservation, you can join a guide from Eagle's Nest Historical Tours for a 35-min tour of the Nest twice daily (5€/person, under 12yr free) starting from the mouth of the tunnel leading to the Nest. *The first tour departs at 10:50 (take the 10:35 bus from Obersalzberg to meet this tour) and the second tour at 11:40 (take the 11:25 bus from Obersalzberg to meet this tour). *Double check times and price before departure.

Weather: Complement your journey to the Eagle's Nest with good weather by planning in advance, i.e. stay on top of the weather reports (either by asking a local or via your favorite online weather site). If you're short on time and get caught on a bad weather day, non-buffs require no more than an hour for a visit, as the views will be doubtful and the place virtually empty.

Restaurant is casual, reasonably priced, and serves traditional and international cuisine. Inside can be crowded and stuffy; consider enjoying your beverage or meal on the outdoor patio. To give you an idea of its prices, a schnitzel (breaded pork cutlet) with fries is 12.90€, spaghetti bolognese 8.60€, large salad 9.30€, goulash soup 6.30€, half liter (bottled) beer from Hofbräuhaus Munich 3.80€, coffee/tea 3.90€, banana split 6.50€.

Band of Brothers: For those of you who caught the last episode "Points," you'll see that Hanks and Spielberg did a superb job of recreating the Eagle's Nest. The only giveaway is when Dick Winters comes up a stairway from Eva Braun's tea room (not possible) and onto the sun terrace to tell the boys they are ordered to hold their present position. The war is over!

Getting to Obersalzberg, (GPS: N47 37.829 E13 02.541). **Railers**, from Berchtesgaden's train station, hop on bus 838 (typically departing mid-May thru mid-Oct daily 9:00, 9:15, 9:45, 10:15, 11:15, 12:15, 13:50, 14:20, 15:10, 16:15, less rest of year) and get off at Dokumentation (10-min ride; small groups consider taxi, about 12€ one way, tel. 08652/4041). From here, the Eagle's Nest bus departure area and cashier are meters away (down the steps). **Drivers, from the** center of Berchtesgaden, pass the pedestrian shopping zone and Hotel Edelweiss (left) and follow the road as it curves right. At the bottom of the hill turn left at the traffic light (direction Salzburg)—this is almost a U-turn. At the next set of lights turn right (route 319, direction Obersalzberg)—upon turning notice the structure to your left; this was the first of many SS checkpoints up to Hitler's neighborhood. **Drivers, if you're** coming from the Austrian border at Marktschellenberg, continue towards Berchtesgaden and after about 5 km follow sign (left, route 319) pointing Obersalzberg. (Moments before the turn, if it's a clear day, you'll be rewarded with a surreal view of Germany's second highest mountain, the Watzmann. Also, just prior to the left turn is the Grassl Enzianbrennerei on the right page 9). **Parking:** There are two parking lots (P1 & P2) neighboring one another at Obersalzberg servicing the Documentation Center and Eagle's Nest departure area. Either lot charges 3€ per day (or 1.50€ with overnight guest card), payable at the nearest automat (Parkschein Automat—push PKW button and put ticket on dashboard of your vehicle). Note that the automat does *not* give change, i.e. bring the exact amount. If lots P1 & P2 are full, drive half a mile (some 800 m) direction Buchenhöhe and park for free at P3 (less than 15-min walk to return).

Hiking to the Nest will take around two hours. Drivers, park at Obersalzberg—Railers, catch bus 838 to Dokumentation at Obersalzberg—hike up the one-way road (the Kehlstein buses take) part way then switch to the marked trail to the Nest. Drivers can also park at the Ofneralm and hike up (90-120 min) or the Scharitzkehl (2.5 to 3 hrs).

EAGLE'S NEST

DO-IT-YOURSELF TOUR,
Eagle's Nest

Bravo! You've just endured a riveting bus ride up the side of an alpine mountain to the Eagle's Nest landing zone at 1,695 m (5,561 ft). Once off the bus, get your ticket stamped with your desired return time at the window to the right. Afterward, proceed to the tunnel. If nature calls, **toilets** are located left of the tunnel entrance as well as in the Nest above.

Tunnel: Before entering the 124 m (407 ft) long tunnel, notice the Baroque-style medallion crowning its entrance: Erbaut (meaning "built") 1938. Now check out the names etched onto the mammoth-sized bronze security doors—many of these soldiers fought their way across Europe from Normandy to the Nest. One of the more legible names, found on the second door left side, is "Stellan Anderson, Rockford, Illinois, 1945, 100th Division." (This tough bunch earned the nickname *Sons of Bitche* in France, winter 1944-45.)

As you march forward to the end of the tunnel, you'll see its interior is made of roughly finished rose-marble blocks, which ring with moisture and encourage the cold. But when VIPs came to visit (such as Hitler and his cronies), the tunnel was comfortably warmed by the dozen or so vents near the floor blowing in heat.

At the end of the 124-meter tunnel the original brass elevator will lift you another 124 meters into the heart of the Eagle's Nest: 45 people in 45 seconds—packed in like a New York subway during rush hour—shoulder to shoulder, face to face, butts against cheeks.

Before you squeeze in, consider the perils of Hitler's chauffeur, SS Colonel Erich Kempka, who had to drive the dictator down this confined passage to the elevator, where Hitler would alight from the vehicle and Kempka was left to manage a smoothly orchestrated return. He would carefully reverse Hitler's dark-blue, 7-liter Mercedes out of the tunnel, then turn the vehicle around and slowly reverse back to the elevator and await Hitler's return. Luckily for Kempka he never had an accident and damaged the vehicle, which would have likely earned him a permanent position on the chain gang at Dachau!

Upon exiting the elevator, step to the right and stop momentarily for a quick **orientation**. With your back to the elevator; if you were to exit the Nest via the doorway to your left and then go right outside you'd arrive at the back patio, but if you were to go left instead you'd connect onto the scenic path/steps descending to the bus departure area (which I recommend you do at the end of your visit if weather permits; allow 20 min).

The hallway in front of you and the rooms running off it are exactly as they were in 1938, except that the kitchen has been modernized to cater to a gaggle of cooks preparing orders for throngs of wanting tourists. To facilitate kitchen staff and food service, management recently made the hallway off-limits to visitors (which, unfortunately, isolates the ex-guards' room last door on the left but you still have access to the **toilets** first on the left). During the Third Reich, guards would assemble in the last room before and after their patrols. When it came to sleeping, guards would retire to the cellar where bunk beds were set up.

Now go through the adjacent (Restaurant) door into the…

EAGLE'S NEST

Eagle's Nest floor plan

= cliff   Map hand-drawn by Brett Harriman
= window
★ = area closed to visitors

sun terrace

Eva Braun's tea room

steps

(Hitler's ex-) ★ office

★ kitchen

oak-paneled banquet room

steps

former conference hall

passageway

outdoor patio

★ hallway

dining room ★

stairs to cellar

men's toilet ★

women's toilet

passage area

elevator

marble fireplace

ex-guards' room ★

walkway

scenic path/steps to buses (20 min)

Oak-Paneled Banquet Room:

As the name suggests, people gather here for a meal (and today it is part of the restaurant). Originally, a long rectangular table spanned the length of the room and could accommodate up to 30 guests. A lavish handmade cloth covered the table that at the time cost upwards of $12,000 to produce. Until recently (2009-10), the only original piece of furniture left in the Nest was a large oak buffet set against the right wall of this room (pictured). All other furnishings were removable and unsurprisingly went walkabout with the liberating soldiers.

At the end of the banquet room six steps drop into the…

Former Conference Hall:

Spearheading the Eagle's Nest is the former conference hall, now a seating area for the restaurant, noticeably the largest room in the structure, featuring five generous windows providing an abundance of light and tantalizing views. The red-marble fireplace is original and still in working order, stoked by more than seven decades of occupants. (Look inside for its birth year.) The multiple imperfections you see on the marbled frame can be attributed to the victorious soldiers in 1945 seeking a piece of history. At this time, much of the floor in the hall was covered with a luxurious, hefty carpet weighing some 600 kg (1,322 lbs). This decorative floor covering was officially cut into small squares and given to the liberating soldiers—a reward justly

deserved. And as *your* justly deserved reward for coming here and being a part of history, walk over to the corner souvenir stand and get your ticket (or book or whatever) rubber stamped for free with a remembrance of the Eagle's Nest; (ask cashier—stamp pictured).

Although Hitler hardly had time for the Nest, (his mistress) Eva Braun did. One of her favorite hangouts is said to be the cozy tea room adjoining the hall.

Eva Braun's Tea Room: Within this intoxicating room
the walls are finished with knotted panels of pinewood that emit a refreshing fragrance suggestive of an evergreen forest. The large picture-frame window at the far side of the room opens to spectacular views of the national park below. Chief among the park's wonders are its sweeping forests of conifers and the Watzmann massif, the second highest mountain in Germany at 2,712 m (8,900 ft), towering above the valley floor resplendent in green meadows and the beautifully blue waters of lake Königssee. (In this room I can't help but feel as if I'm in a capsule hovering above some of God's greatest creations.)

The adjoining doorway leads onto the sun terrace where a pictorial exhibition (in German) focuses on the history of the Eagle's Nest. This is the terrace portrayed in the "Band of Brothers" when Dick Winters informed the boys the German army had capitulated.

When ready, exit via the arched portal at the end of the sun terrace and onto the outdoor patio opening to more eye-popping views. The cross you see atop the meandering trail, marking the peak, has nothing to do with the Nazis. Instead, it was implemented post-war by the local mountaineering club as a remembrance to those who have died while exploring these mountains. If you have time, walk up the stepped trail towards the cross to snap a fine photo of the Nest (like the one heading this Eagle's Nest section or on the front cover of this guidebook). The farther up the trail you go, the better the shot. But for now walk left to the other side of the patio and stand by the wooden railing.

Below is Obersalzberg, and dominating the background is Untersberg mountain. The unique V-shaped crevice you see along its extensive plateau forms the natural border between Germany and Austria. Everything to the left of the crevice and in front of you is Bavaria, everything to its right is Austria, including the city of Salzburg immediately behind and right of the mountain. Virtually the exact vista before you is the final scene in the movie "The Sound of Music" when the von Trapps are seen escaping over the Alps into Switzerland. Now you know they were filmed not far from your present location and thus escaping into Nazi Southern Command. Oops!

That's a wrap, folks! I hope you enjoyed your time at the Eagle's Nest and continue to do so. Note: If for whatever reason you're late and miss your scheduled bus heading back down the mountain to Obersalzberg, don't stress—you'll be wait-listed on the next set of buses, i.e. you will take the place of the person who missed his or her scheduled departure.

Continued from page 11:

Hitler, Paula (b. Jan 21, 1896 — d. June 1, 1960).

Adolf's little sister, Paula, seven years younger than her infamous brother and not connected with his wicked politics, lived in Vienna for many years before moving to Berchtesgaden in the 1950s under the assumed name of Wolff. She never married or had children, keeping much to herself. Until the year 2007 Paula was officially buried in Berchtesgaden's Bergfriedhof, or Mountain Cemetery, but her caretaker must have died because the *lease on her grave was allowed to expire and therefore she was buried over by the new occupants, Hermann and Cornelia Reif. (*Germans essentially rent their plots, typically afforded by family or a dear friend. In Paula's case, the lease on her grave was due about every 12 years. In 2006, payment ceased thereby terminating the lease and effectively opening the site to new burial. My guess is that the Reifs, who died in 2005 and 2006, were her caretakers.) **To get there**, <u>GPS</u>: N47 37.309 E12 59.734, the Bergfriedhof is located across the traffic circle and up the hill from Berchtesgaden's train station. At the far side of the chapel enter the cemetery via the wrought-iron gate, then go right and continue straight on the graveled path, keeping the hedgerow to your right. The former grave site of Paula, now belonging to the Reifs, is in the first group of graves after the hedgerow (second row, fifth grave in). **Note:** Drivers and hikers, not far up the road from the Bergfriedhof is a German military cemetery where 937 soldiers rest from both world wars, (follow signs "Kriegsgräberstätte").

Continued from pages 4 & 6:

Bus 840 to Berchtesgaden (5.30€ one way, 50-min trip) departs typically Mon-Fri 8:15, 9:15, 10:15, 11:15, 13:05, 14:15, 15:15, 16:15, 17:15, 18:15, and Sat/Sun 9:15, 10:15, 11:15, 14:15, 15:15, 17:15 from opposite Salzburg's main train station (by "Forum 1" mall, or from *Mirabellplatz, Rathaus, and Mozartsteg a few minutes later. *Note that at Mirabellplatz there are three different pick-up points—you need to wait at the north end, i.e. the bus stop closest to main train station, but check schedule in advance for changes). If you're planning on returning to Salzburg, **purchase the day ticket** (Tageskarte adult 9.80€, youth 6-14yr 6.20€) from the driver, which will cover all your bus transportation for the day, including to/fro Salzburg and Obersalzberg (bus departure area for Eagle's Nest), as well as to the salt mines and Königssee lake. But if you are a **small group** of 4 or 5 persons, buy the Bayern-Ticket directly from the driver of bus 840 to significantly increase savings. **Note:** Bus 840 terminates at Berchtesgaden's train station, where buses depart roughly every 30 min to Obersalzberg and elsewhere around town. Those of you traveling in a small group of 4 or 5 persons and are planning on buying the Bayern-Ticket from the driver, note that during the week (Mon-Fri) the ticket is officially valid *after* 9:00. The Bayern-Ticket is also valid Sat/Sun but there is neither an 8:15 bus nor an early time restriction on weekends.

Continued from page 4:

Parking Dial: Before hitting the road, make sure you have the nifty parking dial: a small, 24-hour (blue) cardboard disk that is manually rotated and called a Parkscheibe, or often Parkuhr in Austria. With the dial properly displayed on your dashboard you will be permitted to park for free in designated areas.

There should be a dial in the glove box (or in the side-door pocket) of your rental car. If your car did not come with a dial, and you haven't yet left the rental agency, go back in and ask for one. If it's too late, you can purchase a dial cheaply at a gas station or magazine shop. When applicable, a diagram of the dial will be featured on local parking signs along with a maximum time limit, like 1 Std. (short for Stunde meaning "hour"). Rotate the dial to the time you pulled into the space (Ankunftszeit, or arrival time) and put it on the dashboard. This way the parking inspector can see when you arrived and if you've overstayed your welcome.

THE END

meet the author

Brett Harriman

Brett Harriman grew up in the seaside town of Dana Point, California, and was fortunate enough to have parents who dragged their kids with them everywhere they went, including on overseas vacations. Thus, the travel bug kicked in early.

Brett's writings are inspired by his love of travel, to which he has driven across America, trekked around Australia, and explored Europe extensively. Brett lived in Australia for a decade and in Europe for five years, where he was an official tour guide for the U.S. Armed Forces in Germany. In that role, Brett led more than 10,000 servicemen and women and their families through many historically rich cities, towns, villages and Alpine hamlets.

In 2011, for all his hard work, Brett was selected by the president of Oktoberfest to represent the USA during the world-famous festival in Munich, Germany.

When he is not in Europe sleuthing out the latest travel information or on tour promoting *Harriman Travel Books*, Brett spends his time in Pahrump (55 miles west of Las Vegas), Nevada, where his parents have retired and he finds serene sanctuary to compile and compose his travel book series, tour-packages, and publishing business.

Brett Harriman enjoying Oktoberfest in Munich, Germany, September 2013

Pictured insets are of guests on Harriman's Oktoberfest tour packages with the exception of the Munich mayor (bottom left) tapping the first keg

Complement this book with other "Harriman Travel Books" and resources

Every year our brand recognition increases across the world together with our array of destination guides and tour programs.

independent
inexpensive
intelligent

If you're headed to Germany or Austria, let us educate you with local knowledge and history so you can make informed decisions that save time, as well as money, while leading to new adventures and acquaintances abroad.

To minimize the advent of stale news and maximize the value of your dollar, we strive to set the gold standard when gathering research.

Our goal at "Harriman Travel Books" is the trip of your dreams. So come along, your journey begins *now!*

Made in the USA
Lexington, KY
15 June 2014